Herefordshire...
Vision and Verse

Kathleen Freeman

Arrow Valley Publications

Arrow Valley Publications
Church Lane, Eardisland
Herefordshire HR6 9BP
Tel: 01544 388226

Printed by Print Plus: Hereford
Tel: 01432 272025

Copyright © Kathleen and Barry Freeman 2002

All rights reserved. No part of this publication may be reproduced, stored or transmitted, by any means, without the prior permission of Arrow Valley Publications.

ISBN 0 9538081 3 0

ACKNOWLEDGEMENTS

Arrow Valley Publications gratefully acknowledges permission to reprint the following poems:

A P Watt Ltd for The National Trust for Places of Historical Interest or Natural Beauty: *The Way Through the Woods* and *The Glory of the Garden*, Rudyard Kipling.

The Society of Authors: *The West Wind* and *On Eastnor Knoll*, John Masefield; *The Vacant Farmhouse*, Walter de la Mare; *Loveliest of Trees*, A E Housman.

Jonathan Cape Ltd: *The Road Not Taken*, Robert Frost.

Oxford University Press: *De Profundis*, Ivor Gurney.

Andre Deutsch: *Apples*, Laurie Lee.

Secker and Warburg Ltd: *Hedgehog*, Anthony Thwaite; *Swallows*, Andrew Young.

Charter Film Music Ltd: *The Life That I Have*, Leo Marks.

Front cover: A house near Halmonds Frome, which overlooks the Frome Valley.

Facing page: The prospect from Callow Hill on a bright and breezy May morning, looking southwest towards the Black Mountains.

Vignette: Skewbald ponies in an autumn light with Weobley spire in the distance.

The Poems

Page		Page	
8	The West Wind, John Masefield	62	A Wish, Samuel Rogers
10	*From* Britannia, James Thompson	64	The Swallows, Andrew Young
14	To Daffodils, Robert Herrick	70	Hedgehog, Anthony Thwaite
16	Sudden Spring, Gerald Bullett	72	The Return, L. A. G. Strong
18	Bluebells, George Barlow	76	*From* The Barn, Stephen Spender
20	The Mood of May, Richard Edwards	78	The Vacant Farmhouse, Walter de la Mare
24	The Sun Used to Shine, Edward Thomas	80	Duty, Ellen S. Hooper
26	The Donkey, G. K. Chesterton	84	The Rolling English Road, G. K. Chesterton
28	The Way through the Woods, Rudyard Kipling	86	Morning, John Clare
30	Loveliest of Trees, A. E. Housman	88/89	*From* The Brook, Alfred, Lord Tennyson
32	On Eastnor Knoll, John Masefield	90	A Garden Song, Henry Austin Dobson
34	Home Thoughts from Abroad, Robert Browning	92	Thaw, Edward Thomas
34	The Ways of Love, Elizabeth Barrett-Browning	98	The Road not Taken, Robert Frost
36	*From* De Profundis, Ivor Gurney	100	Ode on Solitude, Alexander Pope
38	Apples, Laurie Lee	104	Sonnet XVIII, William Shakespeare
39	A Cider Song, G. K. Chesterton	106	Ploughing up the Pasture, Margaret Stanley-Wrench
42	The Glory of the Garden, Rudyard Kipling	108	Meg Merrilies, John Keats
46	Going Downhill on a Bicycle, Henry Beeching	110	A Birthday, Christina Georgina Rossetti
50	The Old Workman, Thomas Hardy	111	Remember, Christina Georgina Rossetti
52	The Waggon-Maker, John Masefield	112	The Life that I Have, Leo Marks
55	*From* To The Cuckoo, William Wordsworth	114	The Gate of the Year, M. Louise Haskins

A Fresh Look at Herefordshire

It has been exciting to produce this second book on Herefordshire, this time concentrating on some of the less well known but equally interesting and beautiful parts of our county: the Black Mountains foothills; the valleys of the Monnow, Leadon and Frome; and the hidden valley of the Hope Mansell dome, for example. My fresh series of explorations, by car and on foot, have allowed me to discover sights hitherto unknown to me, although I have been familiar with Herefordshire all my life.

There are scenes in these pages from all seasons of the year, the majority photographed specifically for this book between the summers of 2001 and 2002. The poems were chosen by Barry, and I have tried to match either the subject or the mood of each poem as far as possible. The actual compilation of a book is always challenging; maintaining a smooth and logical flow of text and pictures, but aiming to give variety and some surprises as the reader turns the pages.

I love being in the open countryside and try to get out every day, even if only for a local walk, throughout the year: every season has its joys, mysteries and charms. On a January walk near Bromyard I came across an interesting farm with its oast house and, at Avenbury, the ruins of the medieval church, first seen indistinctly through a tangle of branches and undergrowth. The sun is at its weakest of course in early January but, combined with a light dusting of snow, it gave the hills and valleys southeast of Bromyard a magical quality, making a memorable walk.

Memorable, too, was a bright and breezy early May morning when I headed off for south Herefordshire. At the top of Callow Hill my eye was caught by a vast vivid yellow sea of oilseed rape in flower.

Right: In Hergest Croft Gardens

Once I had parked safely and set up the camera, I found myself looking at a panorama to the southwest which stretched way beyond the immediate fields right across to the Black Mountains. Above was a brilliant blue sky, half filled with fast-moving cumulus clouds: some had bases sufficiently dark to promise equally fast-moving, often viciously squally, showers of cold rain. It was on that same day that I took the picture of Goodrich Castle in a narrow window of brilliant sunlight before a storm arrived. On that occasion, as I record in the book, I had to hold the tripod firmly to stop it being blown over.

Such a day is well worth making the best of: I was able to include a distant view of Kerne Bridge, then walk on up to Goodrich church on its hilltop and, having finally lost the waymarked path, came across an unforgettable old caravan in a wood, which I knew at once was the ideal accompaniment to Keats' poem *Meg Merrilies*.

I stressed above parking safely near Callow: sometimes it is a problem. On another excursion in east Herefordshire I came across a freshly ploughed field, its rills making fascinating patterns in the rich red soil of the undulating landscape, There was no convenient verge, so a little further on I reversed into the edge of a wood and began a hazardous walk back to a suitable viewpoint. A high bank one side, a steep drop the other, and blind bends afforded little space to set up my tripod and avoid the fast-moving, heavy traffic. If I hadn't been on my own I doubt if the pictures would have been taken: Barry would have insisted it was far too dangerous.

During other excursions I have been very glad to have Barry with me. When he is driving I can give full attention to surveying the landscape for promising photo opportunities. He also records the location of each set of pictures and tells me what geographical features I am looking at. Most importantly, he makes the tea and deals out the sustenance!

Left: Flower study in Hergest Croft Gardens

Apart from seeking out new places, one meets interesting people. In Bodenham I met Mr and Mrs Perret, who kindly allowed me to photograph their attractive garden and Mr Perret took me across to the hide that overlooks Bodenham Lakes, where I was able to take a good photograph of the sky reflected in the water of the lake. On another occasion a very pleasant lady at Walterstone told me all about the old stone barn she owned, which I had just been photographing. Another person I had the pleasure of meeting was Richard Pim at Westonbury Mill near Pembridge. He has created a delightful water garden around a former mill on the Curl Brook and has now opened it to the public.

There are two people I wished particularly to feature in the book; Leslie Evans at Eardisland and Rosemary Rigby from Wormelow. Both are unique people, with impressive achievements of which they can be justifiably proud. I was glad of the opportunity to photograph each of them in their home settings, and to record how lucky we are to have such personalities in Herefordshire.

Delightful people; beautiful scenery; fascinating buildings: this book has been a pleasure to produce. Barry and I do hope you will enjoy the pictures and poems, and feel that we have again managed to do justice to our peaceful county in this Fresh Look at Herefordshire.

Kathleen Freeman
Eardisland, August 2002.

We are, as always, very grateful to all the staff at Print Plus in Hereford for the quality of this book and, in particular, to John Hewitt for his painstaking attention to detail in the preparation and layout.

Right: A corner of the courtyard at Paunton Court

The West Wind

John Masefield

It's a warm wind, the west wind, full of birds' cries;
I never hear the west wind but tears are in my eyes.
For it comes from the west lands, the old brown hills,
And April's in the west land, and daffodils.

It's a fine land, the west land, for hearts as tired as mine,
Apple orchards blossom there, and the air's like wine.
There is cool green grass there, where men may lie at rest,
And the thrushes are in song there, fluting from the nest.

"Will you not come home, brother? Ye have been long away,
It's April, and blossom time, and white is the may;
And bright is the sun, brother, and warm is the rain, –
Will ye not come home, brother, home to us again?

"The young corn is green, brother, where the rabbits run,
It's blue sky, and white clouds, and warm rain and sun.
It's song to a man's soul, brother, fire to a man's brain,
To hear the wild bees and see the merry spring again.

"Larks are singing in the west, brother, above the green wheat,
So will ye not come home, brother, and rest your tired feet?
I've a balm for bruised hearts, brother, sleep for aching eyes,"
Says the warm wind, the west wind, full of birds' cries.

It's the white road westwards is the road I must tread
To the green grass, the cool grass, and rest for heart and head.
To the violets and the warm hearts and the thrushes' song,
In the fine land, the west land, the land where I belong.

View across to the Black Mountains:
"Where the west wind blows"

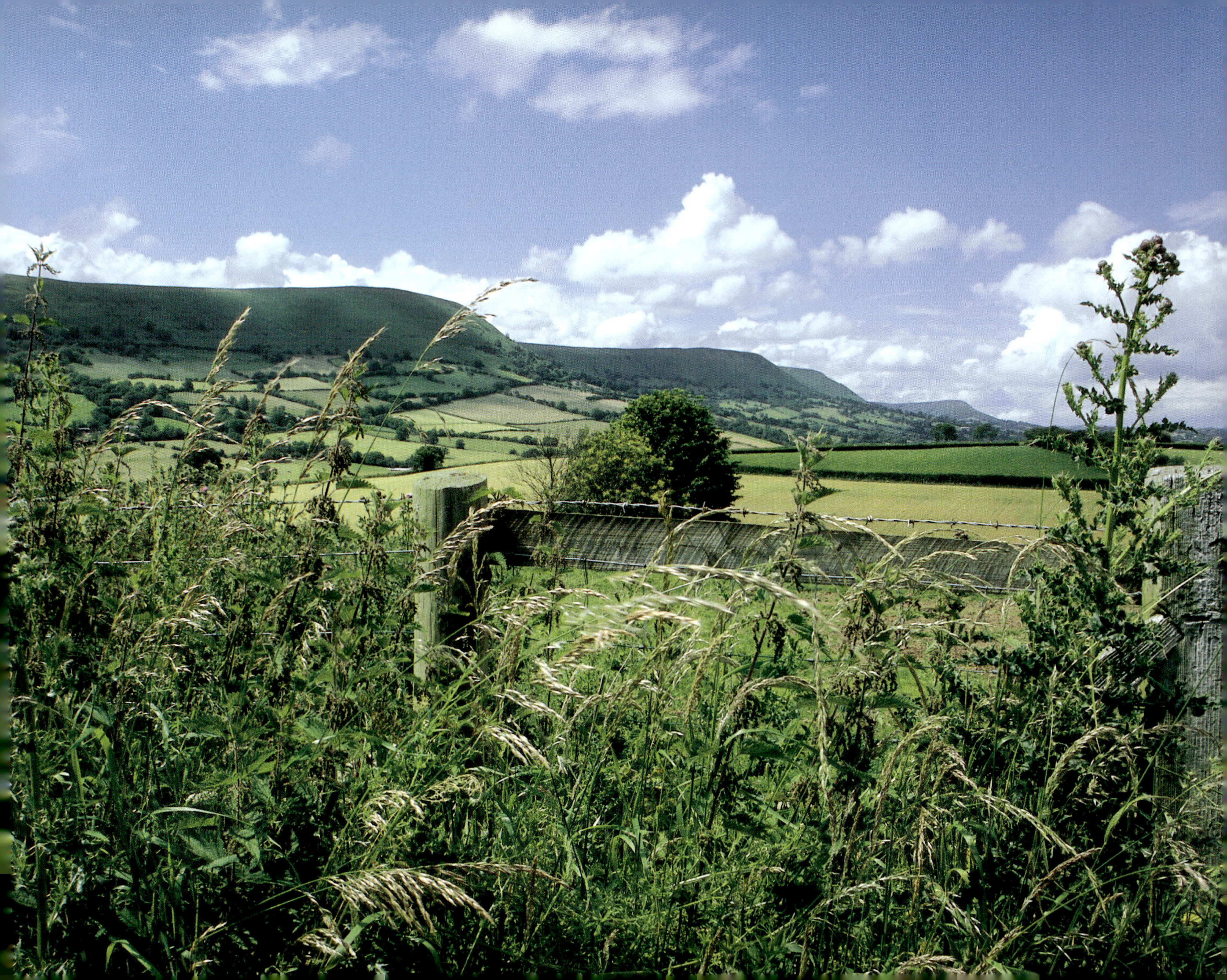

from Britannia

James Thompson

Heavens! what a goodly prospect spreads around,
Of hills, and dales, and woods, and lawns, and spires,
And glittering towns and gilded streams, till all
The stretching landscape into mist decays.

Rich is thy soil, and merciful thy clime;
Thy streams unfailing in the summer's drought;
Unmatched thy guardian oaks; thy valleys float
With golden waves: and, on thy mountain flocks
Bleat numberless; while, roving round their sides,
Bellow the white-faced herds in lusty droves.

The Wye Valley below Kerne Bridge
This scene was taken from a field above Ruardean, just in Gloucestershire, and looking across to Herefordshire. This is where the Wye makes its first cut into the Forest of Dean upland, along the base of Thomas Wood.

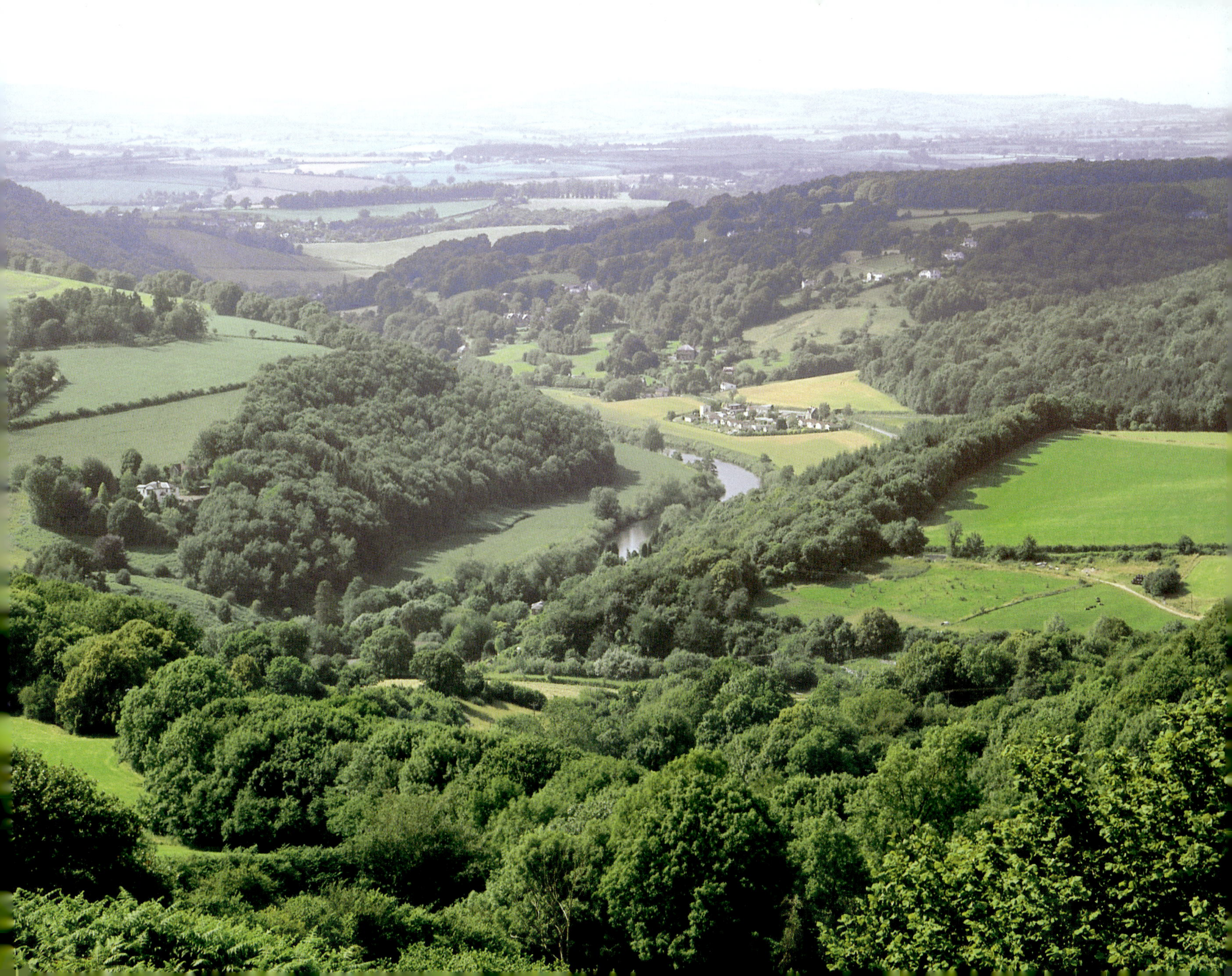

SCENES IN THE SNOW

This page: Two scenes on a walk near Bromyard.

I find the ruined Avenbury church particularly fascinating: I like its sense of mystery and the way nature is steadily reclaiming the site.

Opposite page: The Arrow Valley in mid-winter.

When the sky is blue and the sun is bright, there is colour to record even in the middle of winter, and by using a fairly slow shutter speed I could capture some movement in the water.

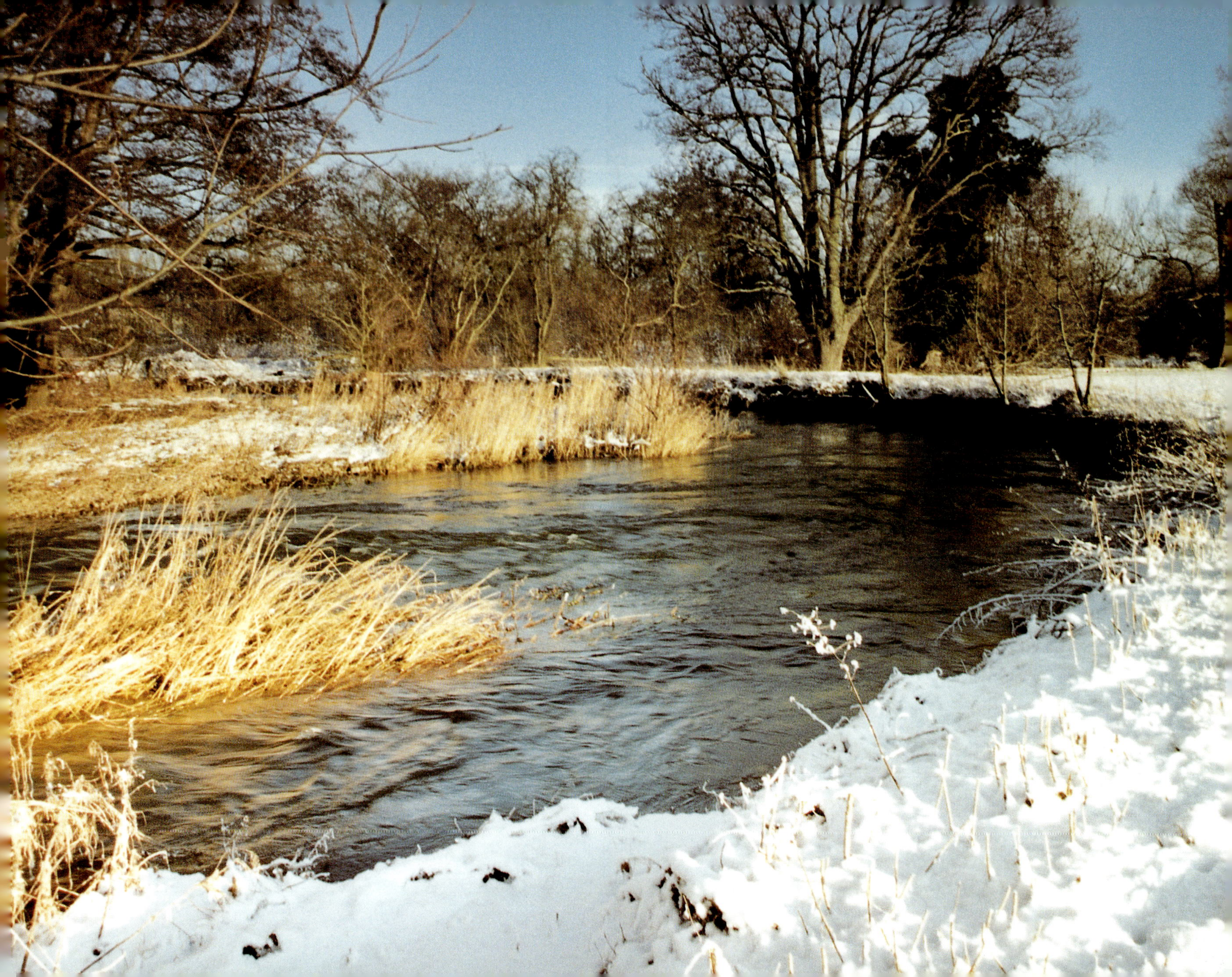

To Daffodils

ROBERT HERRICK

Fair daffodils we weep to see
You haste away so soon;
As yet the early-rising sun
Has not attain'd his noon.
Stay, stay
Until the hasting day
Has run
But to even-song;
And, having pray'd together, we
Will go with you along.

We have short time to stay, as you;
We have as short a spring;
As quick a growth to meet decay,
As you, or any thing.
We die
As your hours do, and dry
Away,
Like to the summer's rain;
Or as pearls of morning's dew,
Ne'er to be found again.

Opposite page: Discovering daffodils.
I met this little girl with her mother in The Weir National Trust garden at Breinton. She was picking her way very carefully through the blooms, lost in enchantment in a sea of yellow.

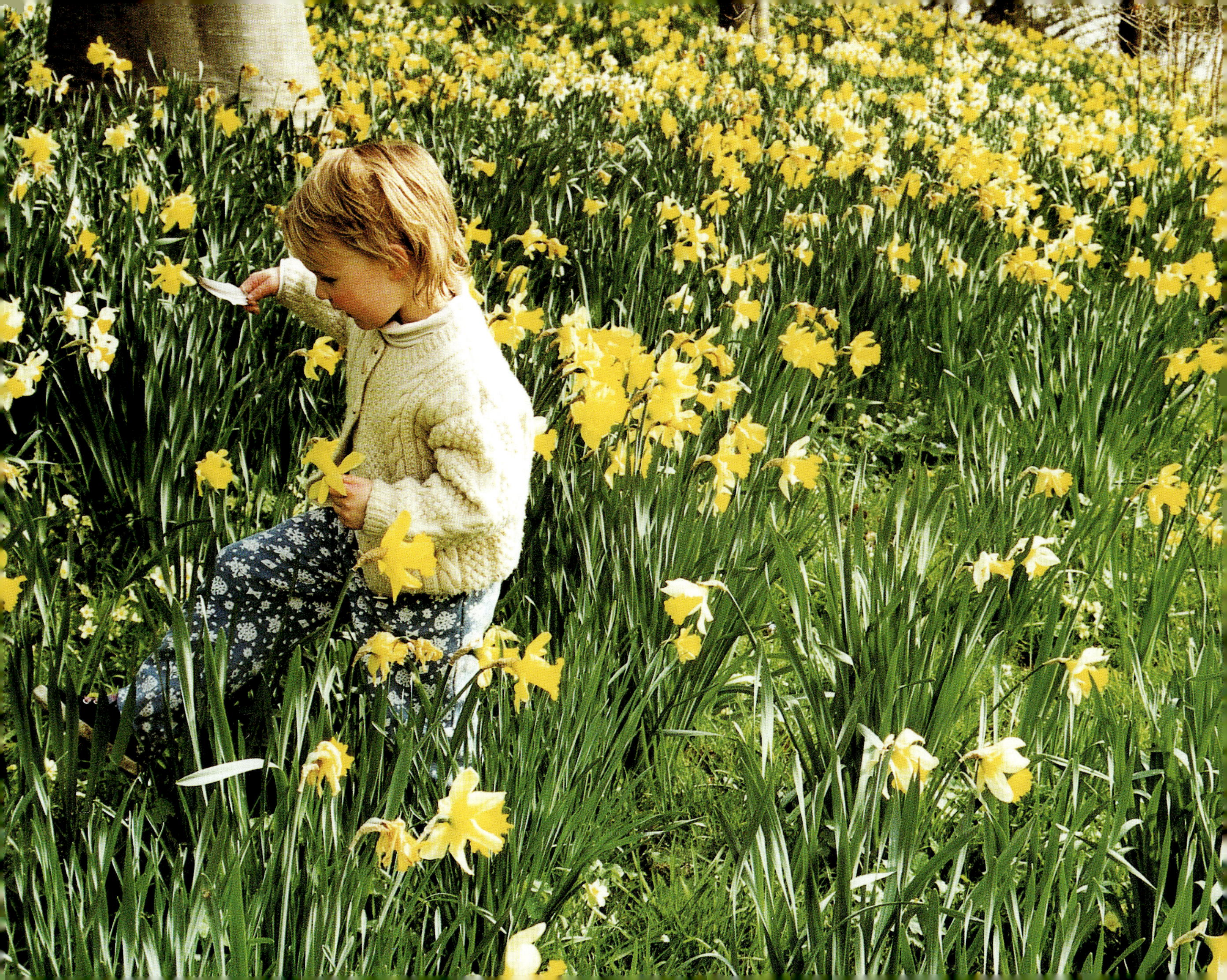

Sudden Spring
Gerald Bullett

Spring is sudden; it is her quality.
However carefully we watch for her,
However long delayed
The green in the winter'd hedge
The almond blossom
The piercing daffodil.
Like a lovely woman late for her appointment
She's suddenly here, taking us unawares.
So beautifully annihilating expectation
That we applaud her punctual arrival.

Opposite page: Early Springtime in the Lugg Valley

This was a striking scene I encountered at Ballsgate Common, upstream from Aymestrey. The snowy blossom of the damson trees contrasted with the rusting roof of the old wooden barn, and the track invites us into the centre of the scene and on to the cottage beyond.

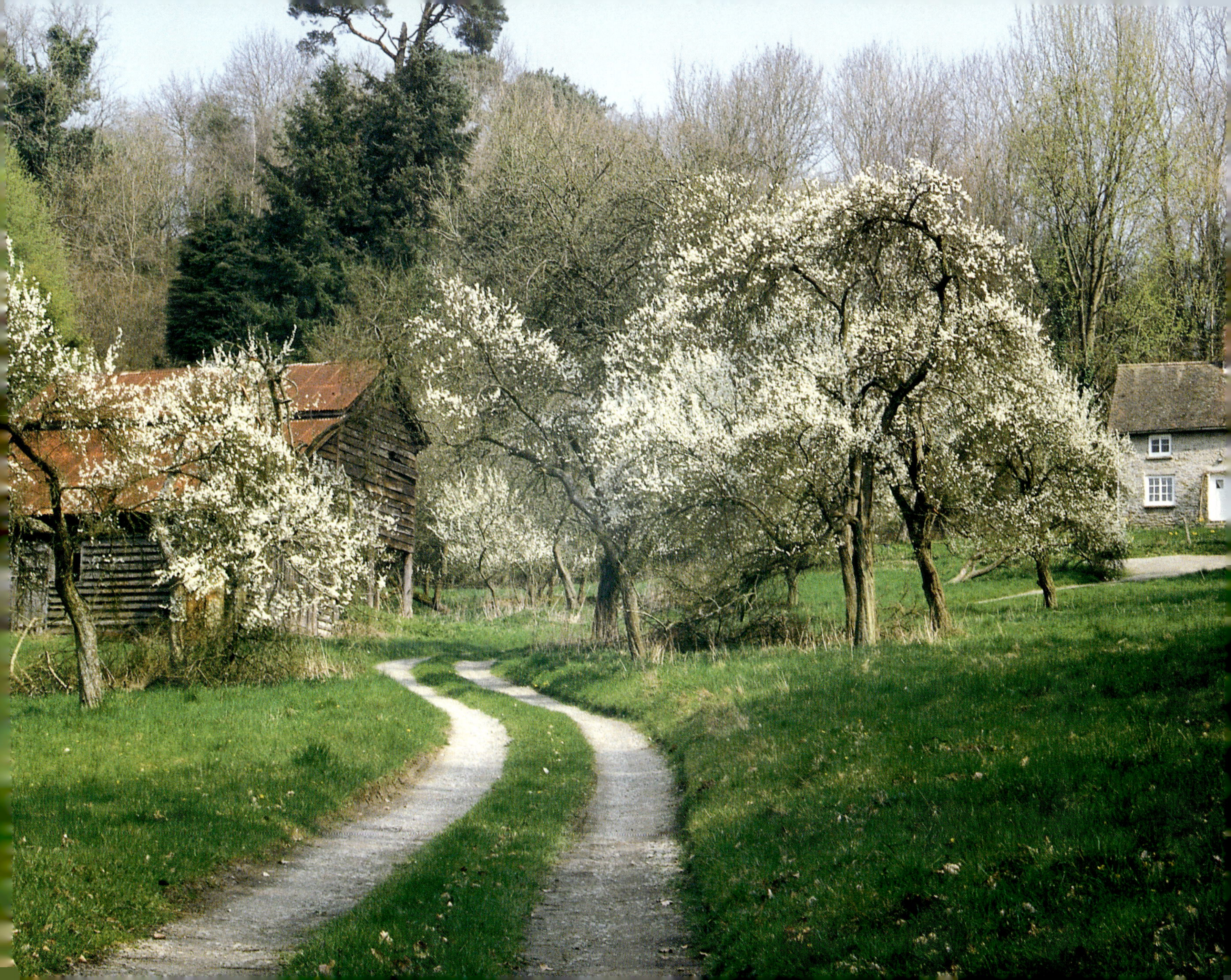

Bluebells

George Barlow

"One day, one day, I'll climb that distant hill
And pick the bluebells there!'
So dreamed the child who lived beside the rill
And breathed the lowland air.
"One day, one day when I am old I'll go
And climb the mountain where the bluebells blow.'

'One day! one day!' The child was now a maid.
A girl with laughing look;
She and her lover sought the valley-glade
Where sang the silver brook.
'One day,' she said, 'love, you and I will go
And reach that far hill where the bluebells blow!'

Years passed. A woman now with wearier eyes
Gazed towards that sunlit hill.
Tall children clustered round her. How time flies!
The bluebells blossomed still,
She'll never gather them! All dreams fade so.
We live and die, and still the bluebells blow.

Opposite page: Bluebell wood near Eastnor.
A bluebell wood is always a joy to come across. I liked the way the tree branches brought the eye down to the path which leads invitingly into the centre of the picture.

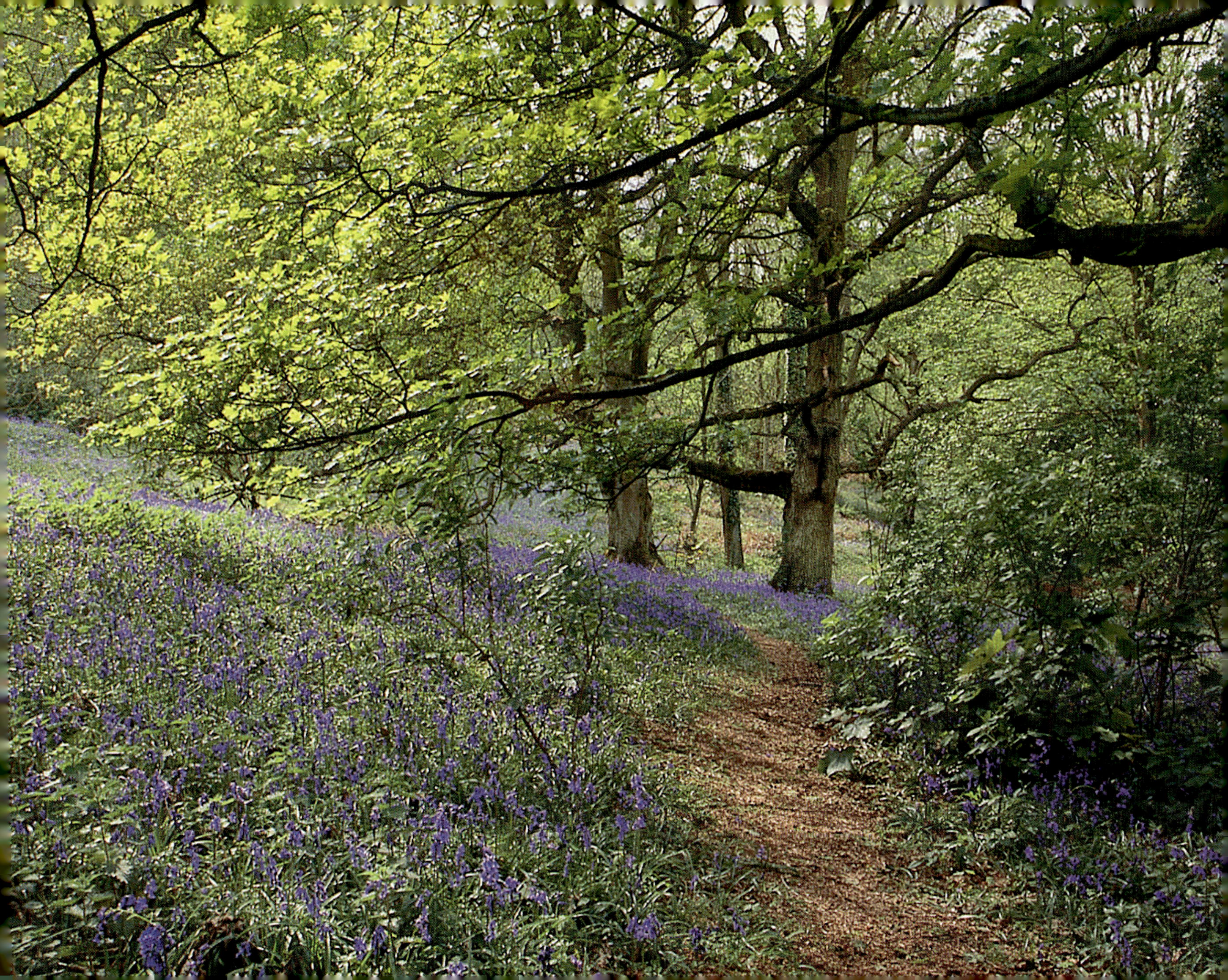

The Mood of May

Richard Edwards

When May is in his prime, then may each heart rejoice:
When May bedecks each branch with green, each bird strains forth his voice.
The lively sap creeps up into the blooming thorn;
The flowers, which cold in prison kept, now laugh the frost to scorn.
All nature's imps triumph whiles joyful May doth last;
When May is gone, of all the year the pleasant time is past.

May makes the cheerful hue, May breeds and brings new blood;
May marcheth throughout every limb, May makes the merry mood.
May pricketh tender hearts their warbling notes to tune;
Full strange it is, yet some we see do make their May in June.
Thus things are strangely wrought whiles joyful May doth last;
Take May in time, when May is gone the pleasant time is past.

All ye that live on earth, and have your May at will,
Rejoice in May, as I do now, and use your May with skill.
Use May while that you may, for May hath but his time,
When all the fruit is gone, it is too late the tree to climb.
Your liking and your lust is fresh whiles May doth last;
When May is gone, of all the year the pleasant time is past.

Opposite page: Impending storm over Goodrich Castle.
In order to achieve this panoramic view I ascended a hill some distance away ... and came face to face with a rather large stag! The day was changeable, with fast-moving cloud banks chasing across the sky in quick succession: it was the same day that I took the Callow Hill picture on page 3.
By the time I had set up my tripod and fitted a sigma 70–210mm lens to pull the image closer, an incredibly strong wind had sprung up, and I had to hold the tripod very firmly to keep it steady. A moment later my lens would have been covered in raindrops but, miraculously, the last burst of sunshine lit up the castle to give a dramatic quality to the whole scene.

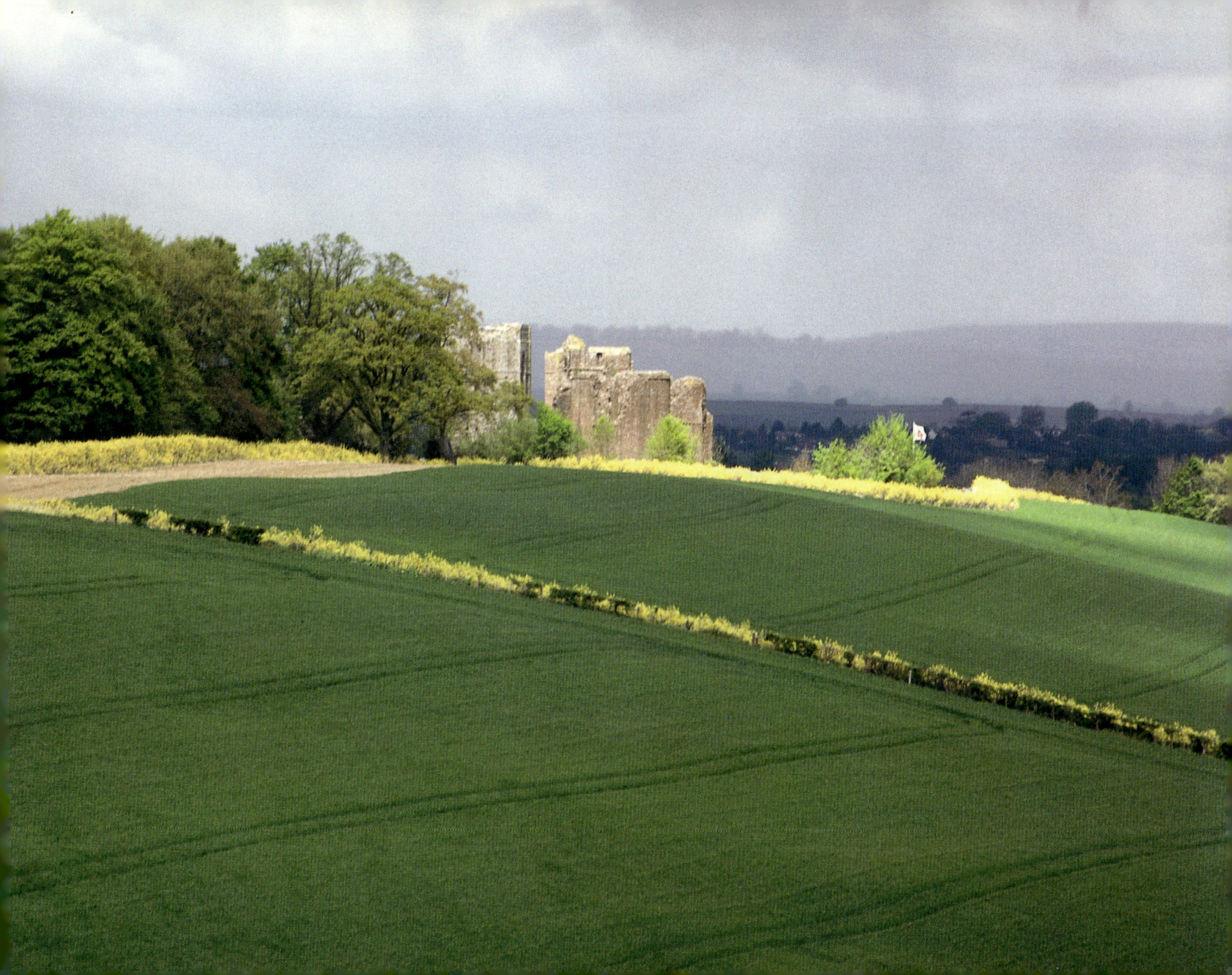

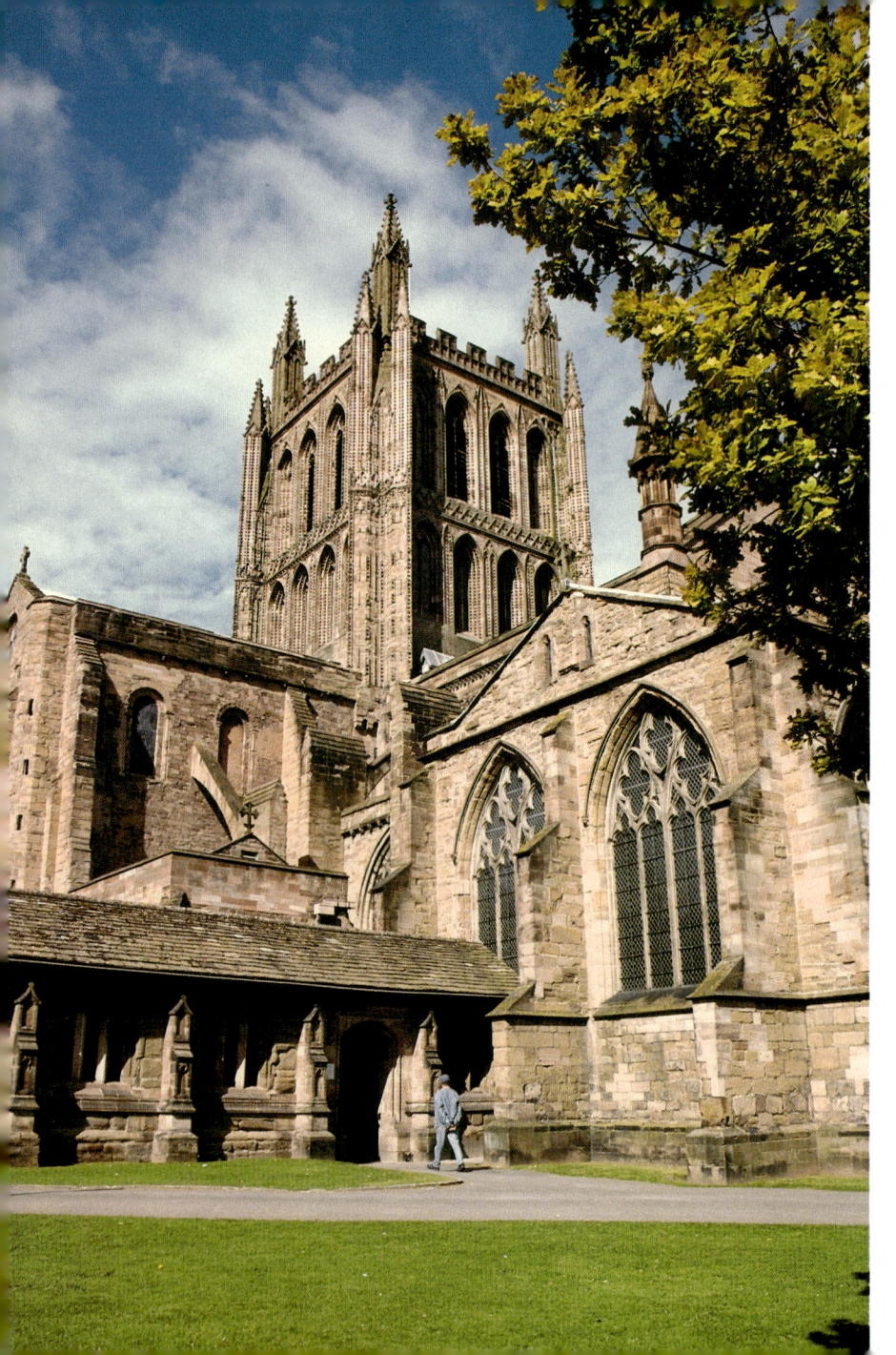

OLD AND NEW IN HEREFORD

A city is a dynamic creation: the art is to retain the best of the old and blend in the new. For any of the nation's twenty-six cathedral cities, the focal point is obviously the cathedral itself, a symbol not only of the city but of the whole surrounding shire.

To illustrate the concept, two views are shown here. I wanted to convey a sense of the awesome bulk of the cathedral building, and chose therefore to get in close to one of its less photographed aspects, the south-east angle surmounted by the tower, outlined against a changing skyscape.

I waited a short time for someone to walk into the scene to give scale and life to an otherwise inanimate building,. The colouring of his clothes fortunately provided a suitable harmony with the sky.

For the wider panorama on the opposite page I chose as my viewpoint the new bridge, Hereford's main structure of the twentieth century. This provided a suitable point for a composition, including another of the city's symbolic structures the medieval bridge, accompanied by the uncompromisingly modern terraced façade of the Left Bank. But still, over it all, towers the great cathedral, as it has for the past seven centuries.

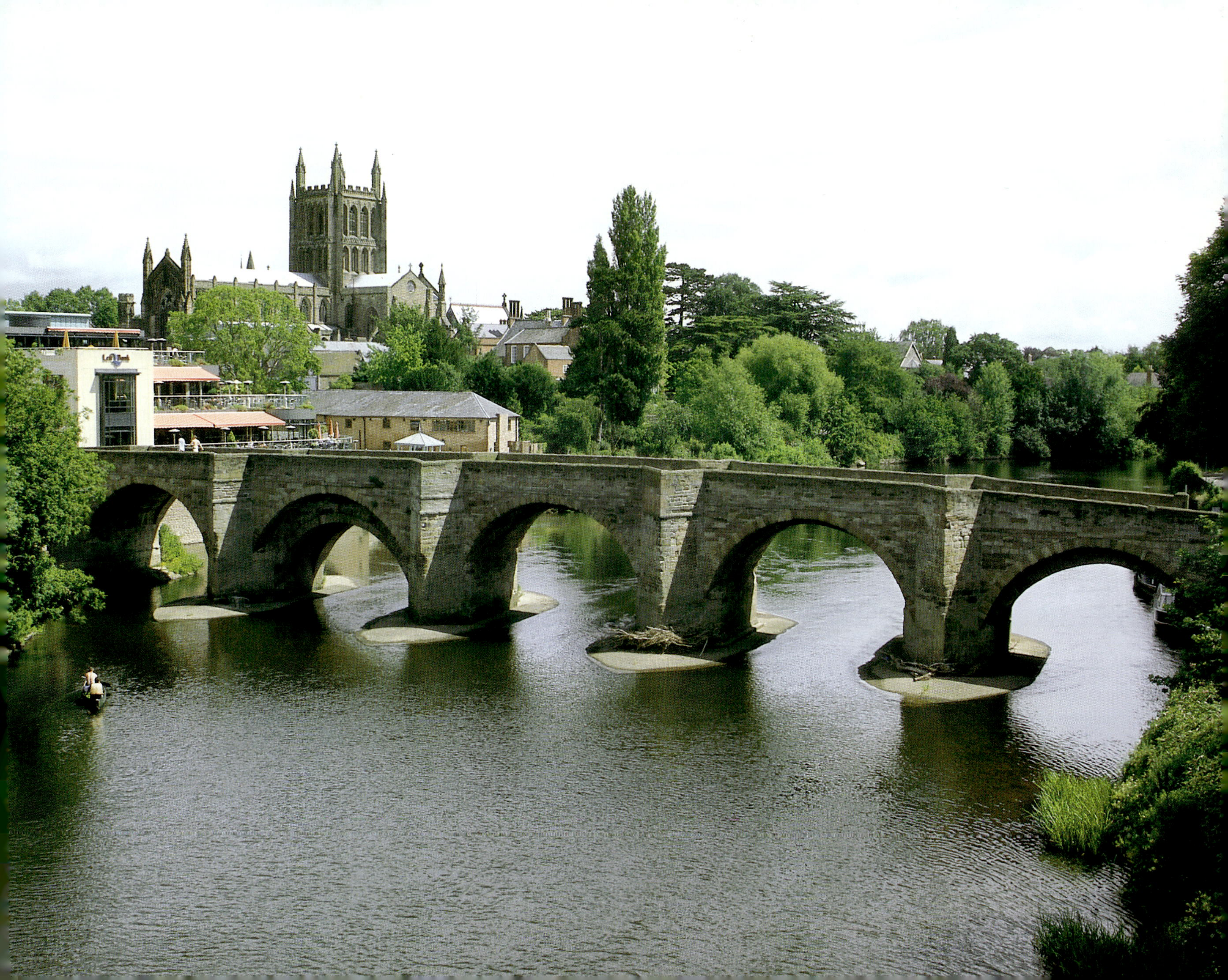

The Sun Used to Shine

Edward Thomas

The sun used to shine while we two walked
Slowly together, paused and started
Again, and sometimes mused, sometimes talked
As either pleased, and cheerfully parted

Each night. We never disagreed
Which gate to rest on. The to be
And the late past we gave small heed.
We turned from men or poetry

To rumours of the war remote
Only till both stood disinclined
For aught but the yellow flavorous coat
Of an apple wasps had undermined;

Or a sentry of dark betonies,
The stateliest of small flowers on earth,
At the forest verge; or crocuses
Pale purple as if they had their birth

In sunless Hades fields. The war
Came back to mind with the moonrise
Which soldiers in the east afar
Beheld then. Nevertheless, our eyes

Could as well imagine the Crusades
Or Caesar's battles. Everything
To faintness, like those rumours fades –
Like the brook's water glistening

Under the moonlight – like those walks
Now – like us two that took them, and
The fallen apples, all the talks
And silences – like memory's sand

When the tide covers it late or soon,
And other men through other flowers
In those fields under the same moon
Go talking and have easy hours.

A Hill Steeped in Poignancy

Mayhill is always a welcome landmark for me: it has been a familiar feature of my mental map of Herefordshire since childhood. It is visible from far and wide throughout the three counties, always unmistakable with its crowning clump of firs.

Apart from my personal fondness for the hill, it is a feature inextricably linked to the Dymock poets, that informal group of like-minded writers who lived and visited in the Dymock area for a few idyllic years prior to the First World War.

It was the briefest of golden ages for English poetry, and the two brightest luminaries were killed. Rupert Brooke died in 1915 on a troopship, after active service in Belgium; Edward Thomas was cut down in a hail of machine gun bullets at Paschendaele in 1917.

Much of the story and a good selection of the best known poems of the six Dymock poets is found in Linda Hart's book, *Once They Lived In Gloucestershire*. Linda used a charcoal sketch of the summit of Mayhill for the front cover of her book.

Edward Thomas and Robert Frost used to take long walks in the fields and on Mayhill: this occasioned Thomas' poem printed opposite. The Dymock poets are all gone now, but we have daffodils all around the village and Mayhill to remind us of those golden years.

Dymock and daffodils and days of song
Before the war had scattered us apart.
    Wilfred Gibson

The picture shows Mayhill above a quiet woodland scene in the extreme south-east corner of Herefordshire.

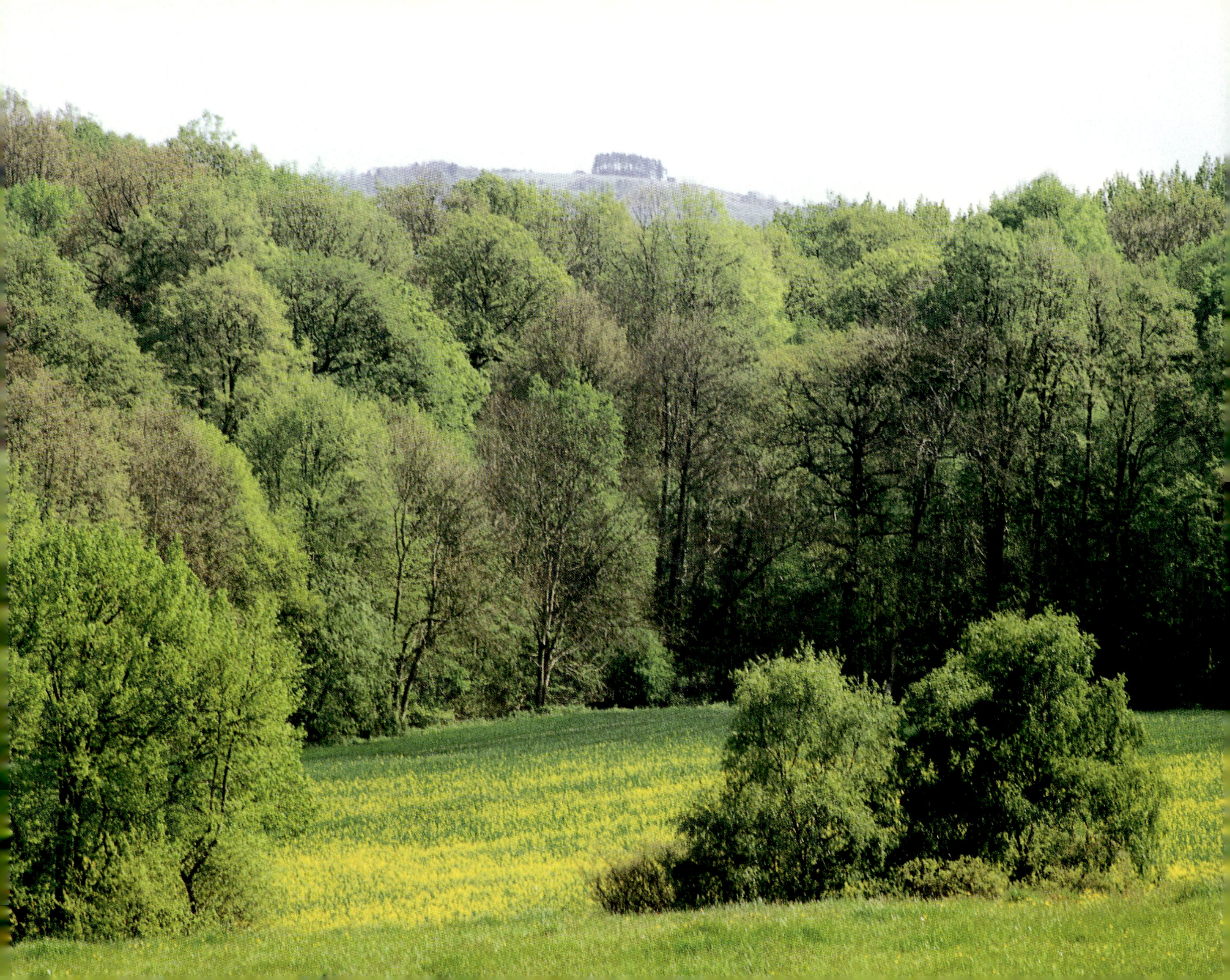

The Donkey

G. K. Chesterton

When fishes flew and forests walked
And figs grew upon thorn,
Some moment when the moon was blood,
Then surely I was born;

With monstrous head and sickening cry
And ears like errant wings,
The devil's walking parody
Of all four-footed things.

The tattered outlaw of the earth,
Of ancient crooked will;
Starve, scourge, deride me: I am dumb,
I keep my secret still.

Fools! For I also had my hour;
One far fierce hour and sweet:
There was a shout about my ears,
And palms before my feet.

A Heavenly Home for Animals

I just had to include these delightful piglets I encountered at Barton Hill Animal Centre, near Kentchurch. I called at the farmhouse seeking permission to take some donkey pictures. They were extremely welcoming and gave me the freedom of the animals' fields and yards.

I followed the freely–roaming piglets into a large barn where they gathered with their siblings. Two greeted each other with a snout-to-snout kiss and, after a few low oink-oinks, they settled down in a long line, two on top of the other four, for a contented afternoon snooze.

We are, I always think, lucky we do not depend on donkeys here as working animals. In poorer countries they are distressingly mistreated: over-worked, under-nourished, their feet and sores untreated. Happily those I photographed at Barton Hill are free to roam and graze in what is definitely a heavenly home for animals.

For visiting details please see Index-Gazetteer at end.

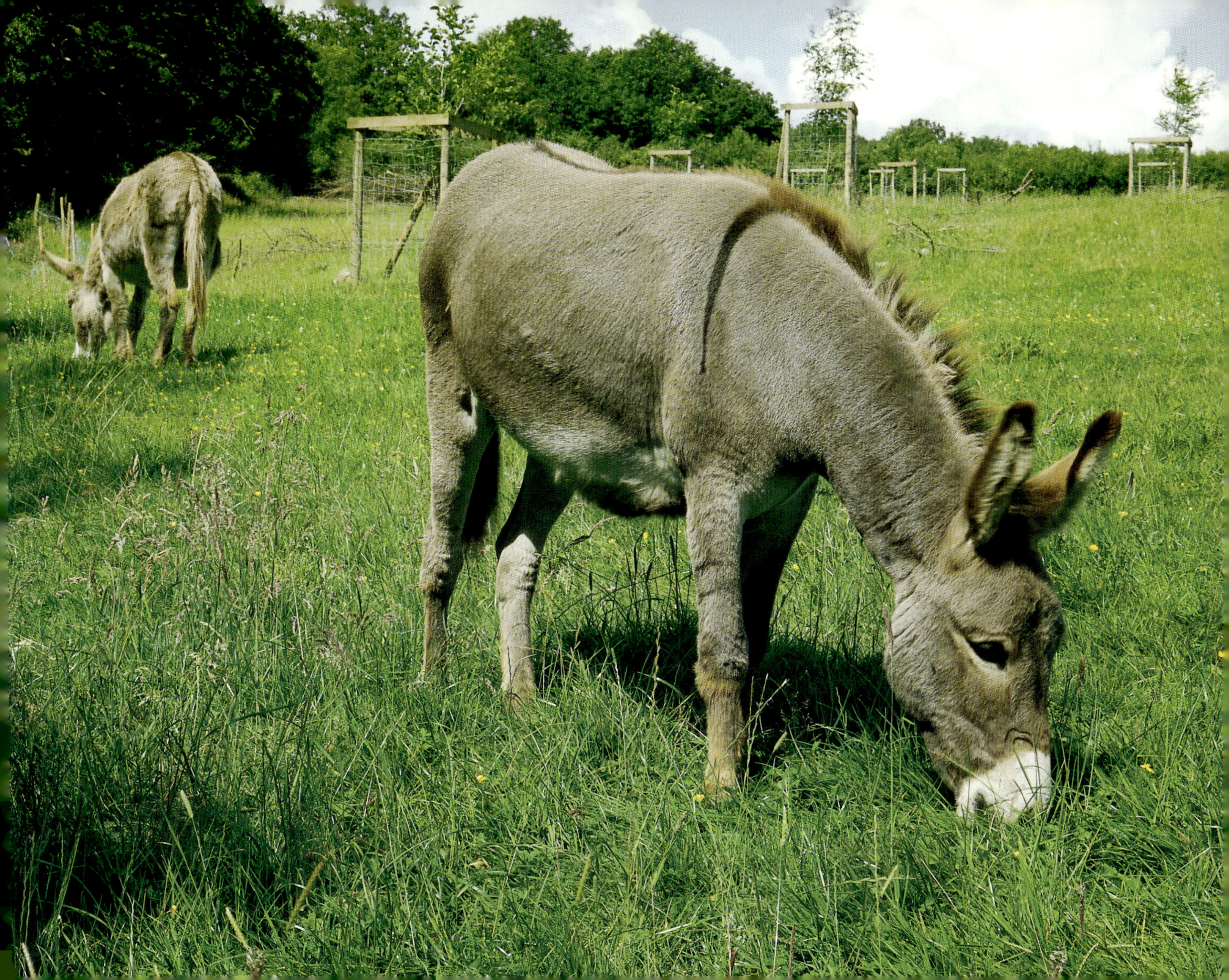

The Way through the Woods
RUDYARD KIPLING

They shut the road through the woods
Seventy years ago.
Weather and rain have undone it again,
And now you would never know
There was once a road through the woods
Before they planted the trees.
It is underneath the coppice and the heath,
And the thin anemones.
Only the keeper sees
That, where the ring-dove broods,
And the badgers roll at ease,
There was once a road through the woods.

Yet, if you enter the woods
Of a summer evening late,
When the night-air cools on the trout-ringed pools
Where the otter whistles his mate,
(They fear not men in the woods,
Because they see so few.)
You will hear the beat of a horse's feet,
And the swish of a skirt in the dew,

Steadily cantering through
The misty solitudes,
As though they perfectly knew
The old lost road through the woods …
But there is no road through the woods.

Above: Woodland Edge
Sunlight behind and on the leaves gave this scene a certain air of serene mystery.

Opposite page: Woodland and Clouds above Goodrich
I was attracted to this uncomplicated scene on a breezy day in May. I particularly wanted to capture the pattern of cumulus building up behind, and replicating the tops of the line of trees.

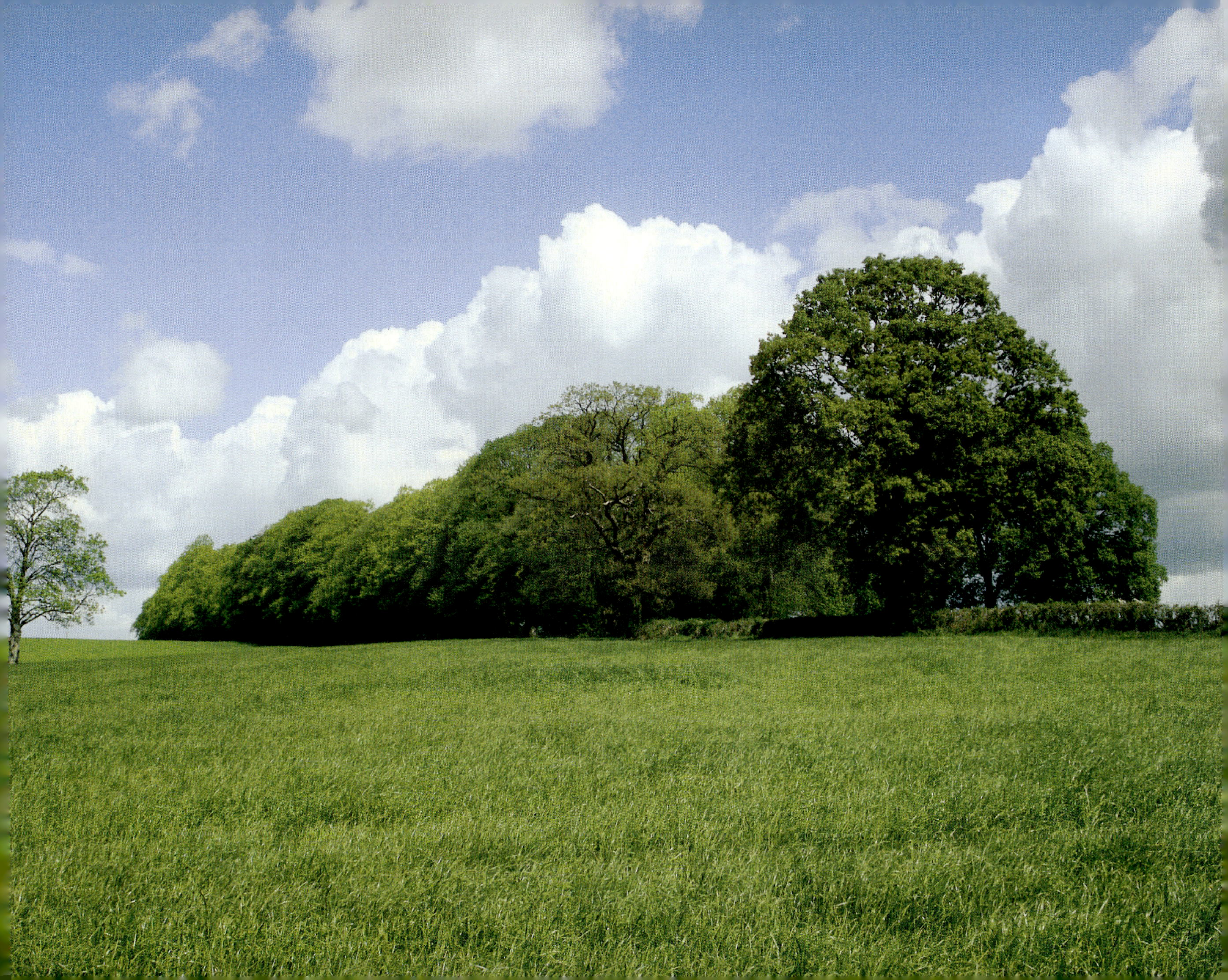

Loveliest of Trees …
A. E. HOUSMAN

Loveliest of trees, the cherry now
Is hung with bloom along the bough,
And stands about the woodland ride
Wearing white for Eastertide.

Now, of my three score years and ten,
Twenty will not come again,
And take from seventy years a score,
It only leaves me fifty more.

And since to look at things in bloom
Fifty springs leave little room,
About the woodlands will I go
To see the cherry hung with snow.

Springtime is Blossom Time
Right: On Bringsty Common, near Bromyard.
Opposite: In an orchard at Holme Lacy.

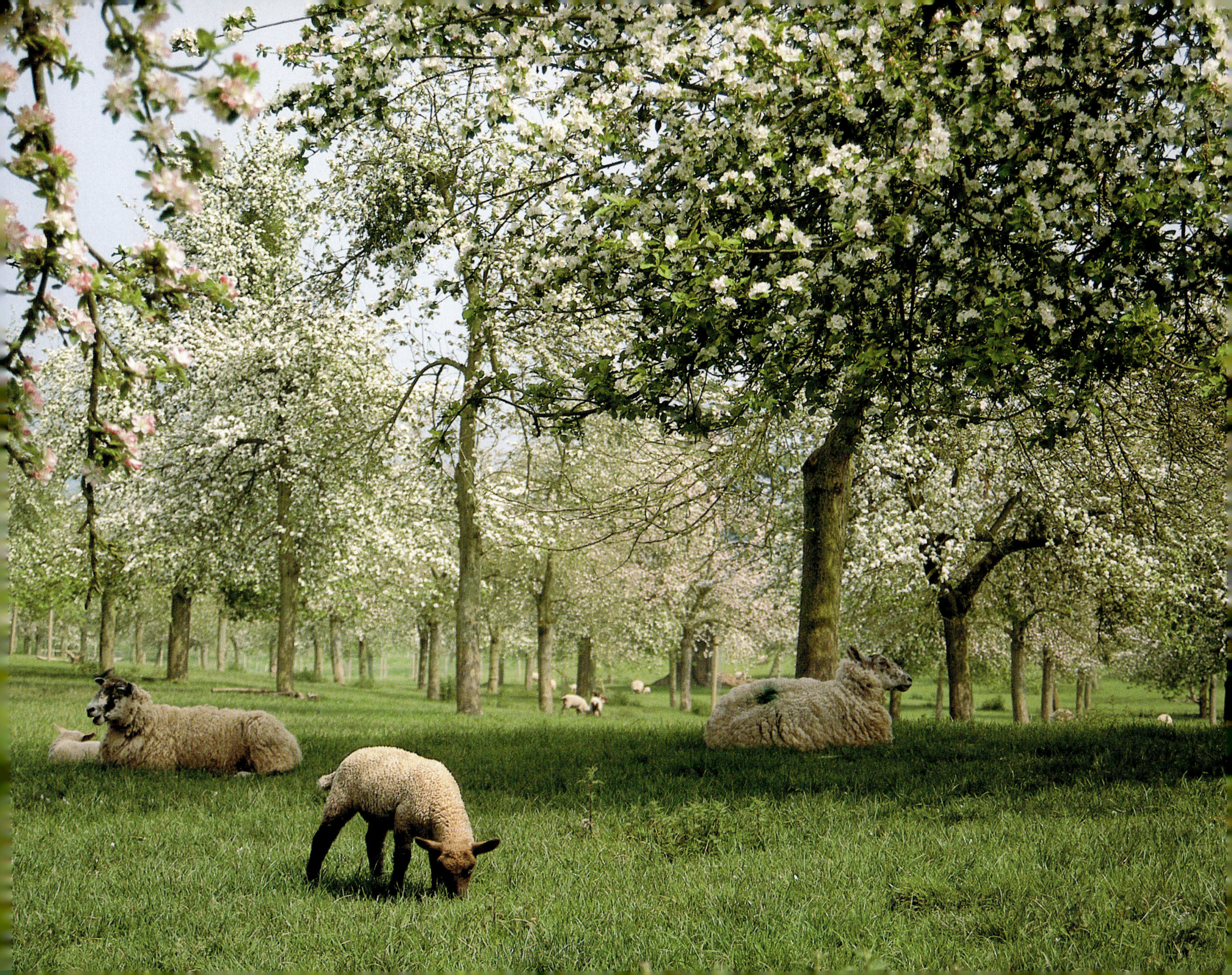

On Eastnor Knoll

John Masefield

Silent are the woods, and the dim green boughs are
Hushed in the twilight: yonder, in the path through
The apple-orchard, is a tired plough-boy
Calling the cows home.

A bright white star blinks, the pale moon rounds, but
Still the red, lurid wreckage of the sunset
Smoulders in smoky fire, and burns on
The misty hill-tops.

Ghostly it grows, and darker, the burning
Fades into smoke, and now the gusty oaks are
A silent army of phantoms thronging
A land of shadows.

LANDMARKS ABOVE THE ROOFTOPS

Ledbury's two tallest buildings seen above the neighbouring rooftops: the spire of St Michael and All Angels, 200 feet high and crowning the county's most majestic bell tower and the Victorian gothic clock tower of the Barrett-Browning Institute looking down on the St Katherine almshouses, restored in the nineteenth century.

OF POETS AND LEDBURY

John Masefield, a former Poet Laureate, was born and spent his early years in Ledbury. In recent years Ledbury Poetry Festival has become established among the country's most significant annual literary events.

The association of Ledbury with poetry however reaches back further, well into the nineteenth century, and was occasioned by one of the great love stories of English literature: Elizabeth Barrett and Robert Browning.

Colwall, on the western slopes of the Malverns, was the scene of the happy childhood of Elizabeth Barrett, before a riding injury and changed family circumstances cruelly ended her carefree years. Her father took the now invalid Elizabeth to London, where she was virtually confined to their house in Wimpole Street.

Despite her father's protective and possessive nature, Robert Browning began to visit Elizabeth, and eventually she escaped virtual home imprisonment by eloping with him to Italy. There she regained her happiness and flourished as a fairly widely-read poet of the mid-Victorian period.

Ledbury commemorated Elizabeth Barrett-Browning by naming the new educational institute after her in the 1890's. The town's high school is named after John Masefield. On these four pages are pictures and poems to record the now long-established association between Ledbury and poetry.

Home Thoughts from Abroad
Robert Browning

Oh, to be in England
Now that April's there.
And whoever wakes in England
Sees. some morning, unaware,
That the lowest boughs and the brushwood sheaf
Round the elm-tree bole are in tiny leaf,
While the chaffinch sings on the orchard bough
In England – now!
And after April, when May follows,
And the whitethroat builds, and all the swallows!
Hark, where my blossomed pear-tree in the hedge
Leans to the field and scatters on the clover
Blossoms and dewdrops – at the bent spray's edge
That's the wise thrush; he sings each song twice over,
Lest you should think he never could recapture
The first fine careless rapture!
And though the fields look rough with hoary dew,
All will be gay when noontide wakes anew
The buttercups, the little children's dower
Far brighter than this gaudy melon-flower.

The Ways of Love
Elizabeth Barrett Browning

How do I love thee? Let me count the ways.
I love thee to the depth and breadth and height
My soul can reach, when feeling out of sight
For the ends of Being and ideal Grace.
I love thee to the level of every day's
Most quiet need, by sun and candlelight.
I love thee freely, as men strive for Right:
I love thee purely, as they turn from Praise.
I love thee with the passion put to use
In my old griefs, and with my childhood's faith.
I love thee with a love I seemed to lose
With my lost saints, – I love thee with the breath,
Smiles, tears, of all my life! – and, if God choose,
I shall but love thee better after death.

Looking across the Frome Valley to the Malverns
This view was chosen to complement the two poems above: here we see the English countryside clad in the lush greens of early summer and look across to the western slopes of the Malvern Hills above Colwall where the young Elizabeth Barrett enjoyed so many carefree pony rides before her tragic accident.

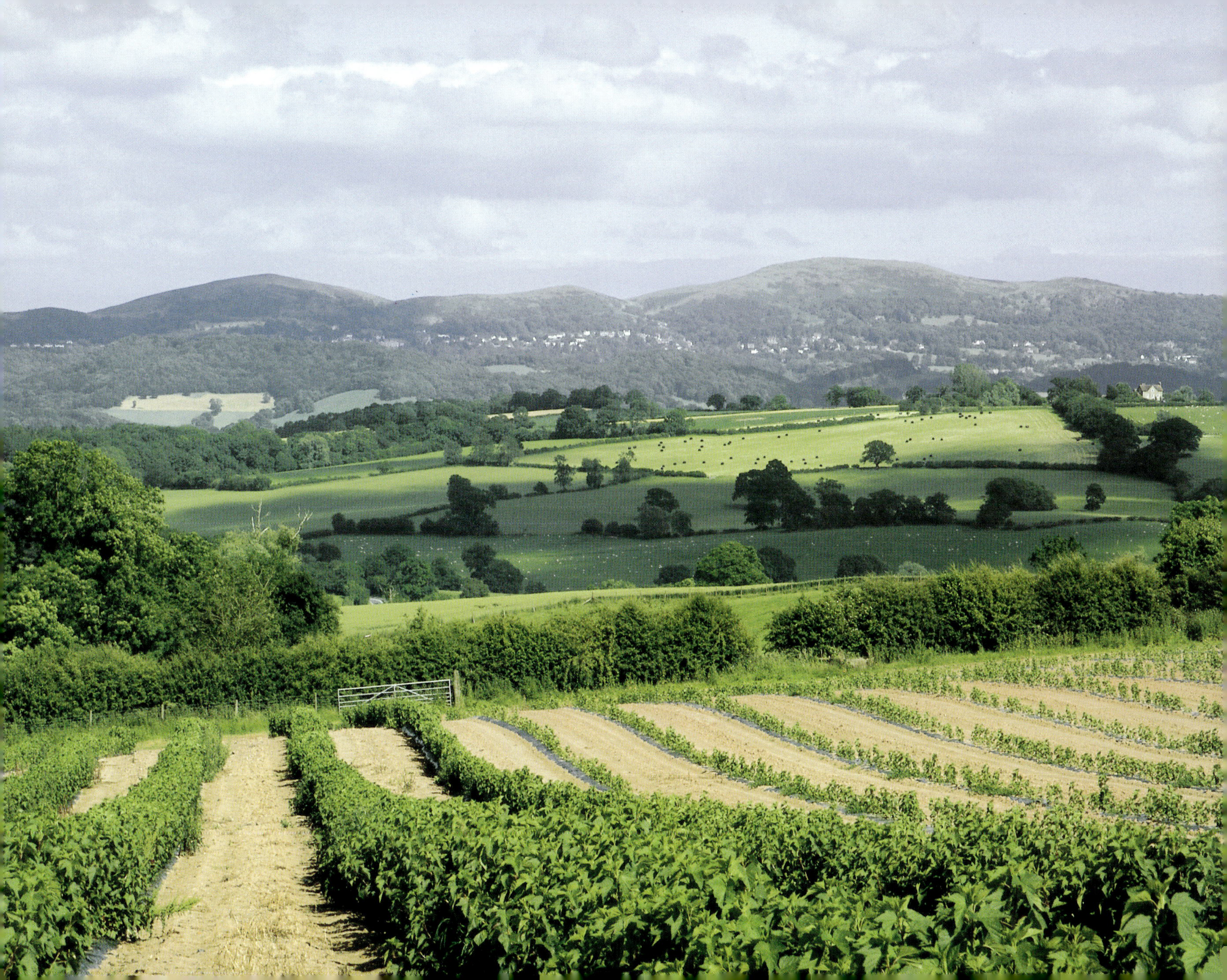

From De Profundis

Ivor Gurney

If only this fear would leave me I could dream of Crickley Hill,
And a hundred thousand thoughts of home would visit my heart in sleep;
But here the peace is shattered all day by the devil's will,
And the guns bark night-long to spoil the velvet silence deep.

O who could think that once we drank in quiet inns and cool
And saw brown oxen trooping the dry sands to slake
Their thirst at the river flowing, or plunged in silver pool
To shake the sleepy drowse off before well awake?

We are stale here, we are covered body and soul and mind
With mire of the trenches, close clinging and foul.
We have left our old inheritance, our Paradise behind,
And clarity is lost to us and cleanness of soul.

Autumn will be here soon, but the road of coloured leaves
Is not for us, the up and down highway where go
Earth's pilgrims to wonder where Malvern upheaves
That blue-emerald splendour under great clouds of snow.

Some day we'll fill in trenches, level the land and turn
Once more joyful faces to the country where trees
Bear thickly for good drink, where strong sunsets burn
Huge bonfires of glory – O God send us peace

Hard it is for men of moors or fens to endure
Exile and hardship, or the northland grey-drear:
But we of the rich plain of sweet airs and pure,
Oh! Death would take so much from us, how should we not fear?

A MAN SHATTERED

This is a powerful poem from a Gloucestershire man enduring the worst conditions men have ever had to endure. Ivor Gurney was wounded, gassed, and mentally shattered. Here he contrasts the scenes of the trenches with his earlier years in the western shires.

To provide some sense of the visions Gurney had of his homeland, two essentially tranquil scenes are selected: above is a view of the Black Mountains from a gateway at Wigga, near Rowlestone; opposite is a summer's evening view of Titley church near Kington.

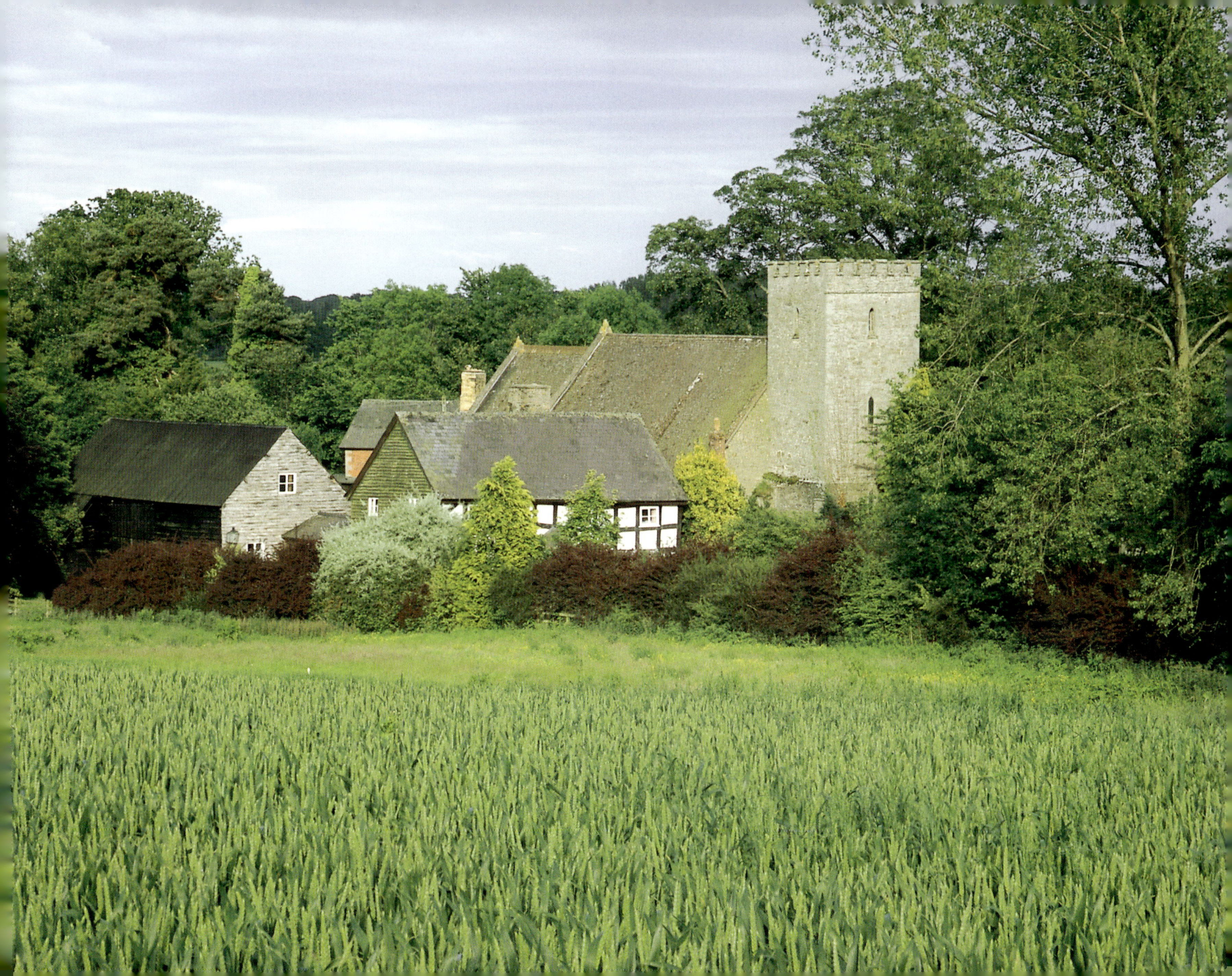

Apples
Laurie Lee

Behold the apples' rounded worlds:
juice-green of July rain,
the black polestar of flower, the rind
mapped with its crimson stain.

The russet, crab and cottage red
burn to the sun's hot brass,
then drop like sweat from every branch
and bubble in the grass.

They lie as wanton as they fall
and when they fall they break,
the stallion clamps his crunching jaws,
the starling stabs his beak.

In each plump gourd the cidery bite
of boys' teeth tears the skin;
the waltzing wasp consumes his share,
the bent worm enters in.

I, with an easy hunger, take
entire my season's dole;
welcome the ripe, the sweet, the sour,
the hollow and the whole.

A Cider Song
G. K. CHESTERTON

The wine they drink in Paradise
They make in Haute Lorraine;
God brought it burning from the sod
To be a sign and signal rod
That they that drink the blood of God
Shall never thirst again.

The wine they praise in Paradise
They make in Ponterey,
The purple wine of Paradise,
But we have better at the price;
It's wine they praise in Paradise,
It's cider that they pray.

The wine they want in Paradise
They find in Plodder's End,
The apple wine of Hereford,
Of Hafod Hill and Hereford,
Where woods went down to Hereford,
And there I had a friend.

The soft feet of the blessed go
In the soft western vales,
The road the silent saints accord,
The road from Heaven to Hereford
Where the apple wood of Hereford
Goes all the way to Wales.

The New Gardens at Hampton Court

Whatever images one selects it is not possible to do full justice to this magnificent new garden. Its opening to the public has been an event of much more than county importance: it is a significant addition to the national stock of country properties for us all to enjoy.

Here is one of Herefordshire's most important country estates in a superb setting, looking across meadowland to the River Lugg, where it curves along the northern flank of Dinmore Hill, providing opportunities for hitherto inaccessible riverside and woodland walks.

I have chosen three images to convey a sense of the garden's variety, and to complement Kipling's classic poem *The Glory of the Garden*. On this page we see part of the long herbaceous border leading to the Dutch Garden with its canal and picturesque summer house.

Opposite is one of a pair of island pavilions located within a system of linked canals and rills. I selected a viewpoint to emphasise the tonal harmony between the extensive flower beds and the clearly defined structural geometry of the pavilion.

Overleaf is the sunken garden, and above it the Gothic tower in the centre of the maze (where I got lost!). From the top of the tower is a panoramic view of the whole garden; from its base a secret tunnel leads to the sunken garden.

For the opening times of Hampton Court Gardens, please see the Index and Gazetteer.

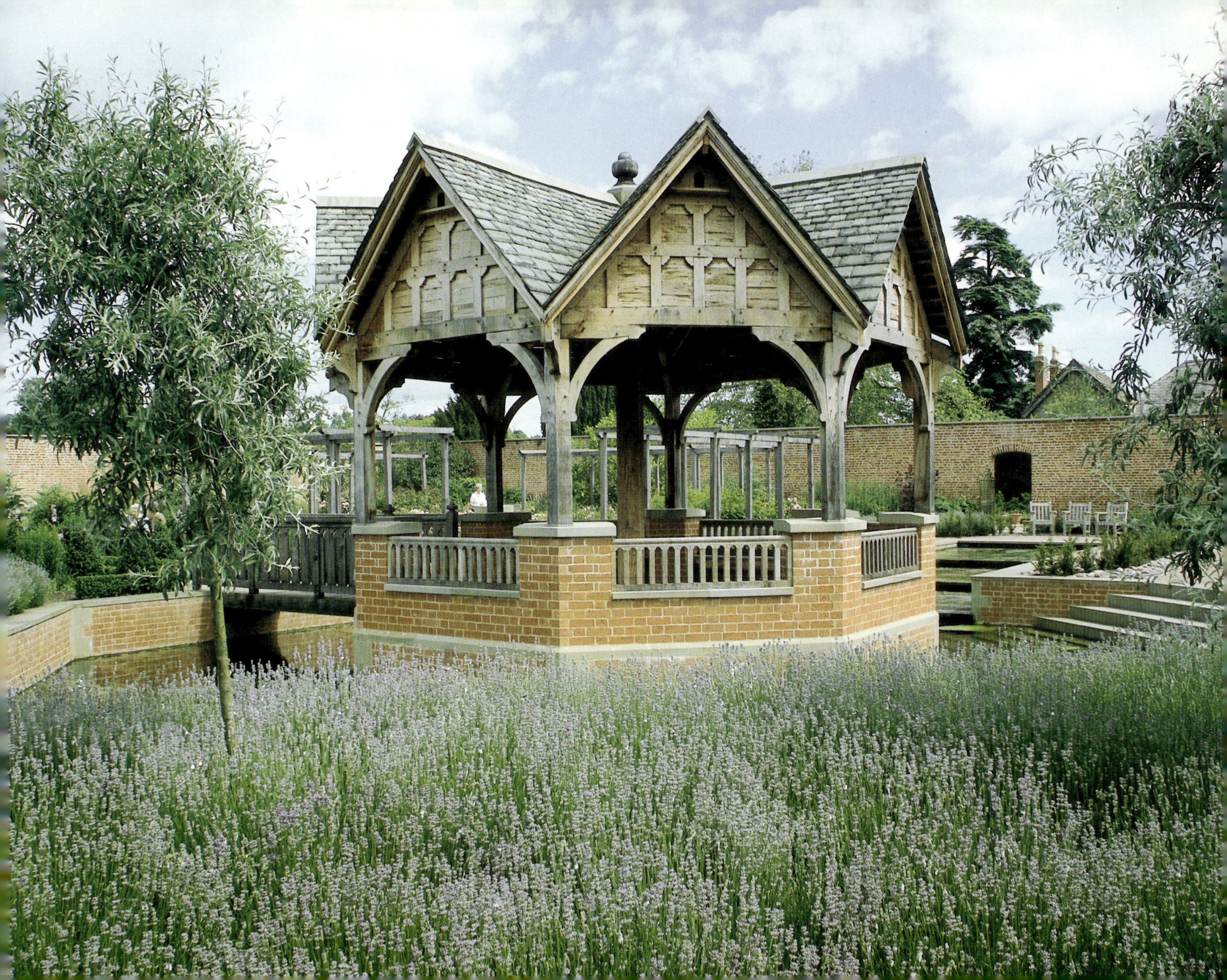

The Glory of the Garden

Rudyard Kipling

Our England is a garden that is full of stately views.
Of borders, beds and shrubberies and lawns and avenues.
With statues on the terraces and peacocks strutting by:
But the Glory of the Garden lies in more than meets the eye.

For where the old thick laurels grow, along the thin red wall,
You find the tool- and potting-sheds which are the heart of all;
The cold-frames and the hot-houses, the dungpits and the tanks,
The rollers, carts and drain-pipes, with the barrows and the planks.

And there you'll see the gardeners, the men and 'prentice boys
Told off to do as they are bid and do it without noise:
For, except when seeds are planted and we shout to scare the birds.
The Glory of the Garden it abideth not in words.

And some can pot begonias and some can bud a rose,
And some are hardly fit to trust with anything that grows;
But they can roll and trim the lawns and sift the sand and loam.
For the Glory of the Garden occupieth all who come.

Our England is a garden, and such gardens are not made
By singing – 'Oh, how beautiful!' and sitting in the shade,
While better men than we go out and start their working lives
At grubbing weeds from gravel-paths with broken dinner-knives.

There's not a pair of legs so thin, there's not a head so thick,
There's not a hand so weak and white, nor yet a heart so sick,
But it can find some needful job that's crying to be done,
For the Glory of the Garden glorifieth every one.

Then seek your job with thankfulness and work till further orders,
If it's only netting strawberries or killing slugs on borders:
And when your back stops aching and your hands begin to harden,
You will find yourself a partner in the Glory of the Garden.

Oh, Adam was a gardener, and God who made him sees
That half a proper gardener's work is done upon his knees.
So when your work is finished, you can wash your hands and pray
For the Glory of the Garden, that it may not pass away!

And the Glory of the Garden it shall never pass away!

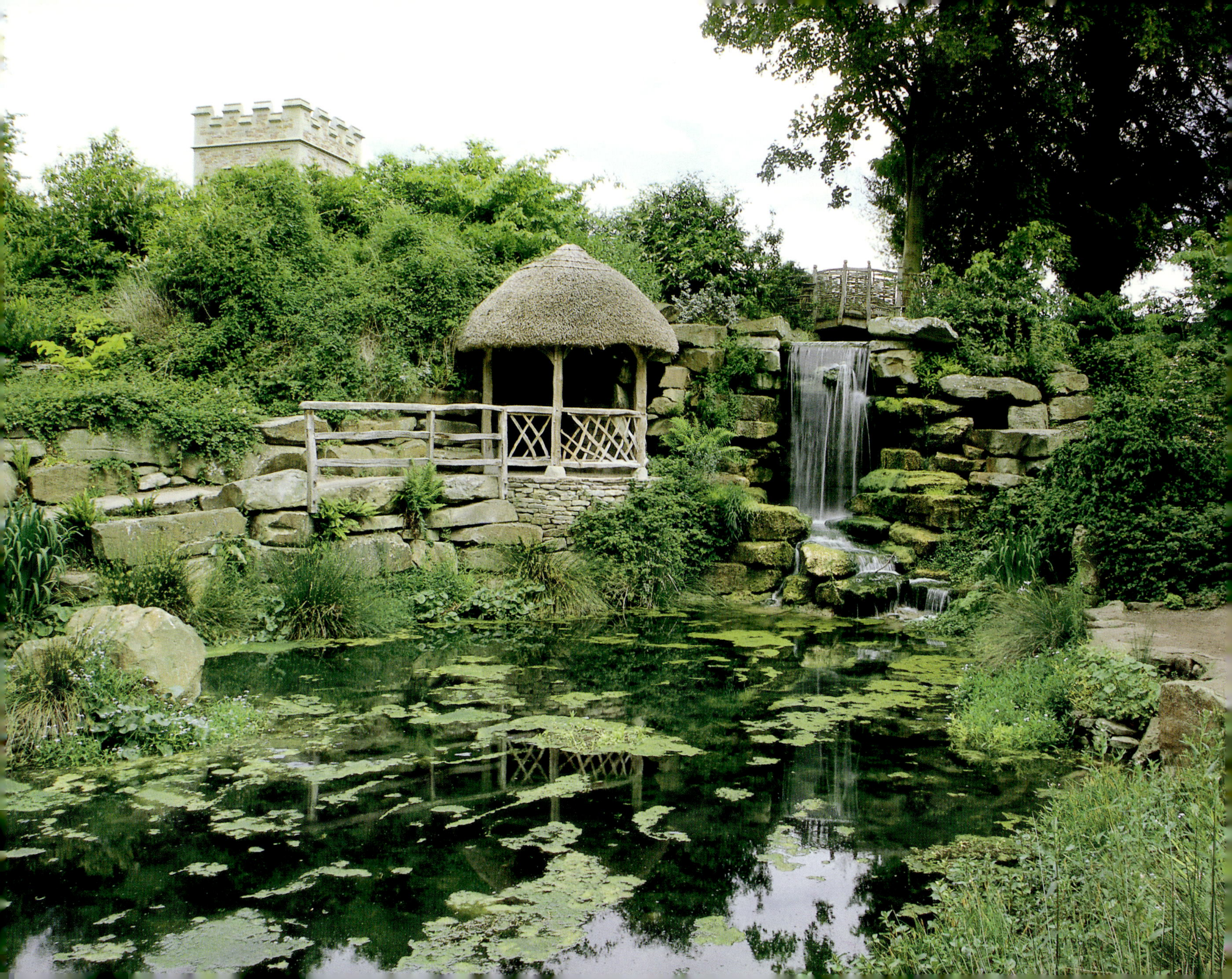

WESTONBURY MILL WATER GARDEN

This is another delightful garden, newly created, which has been opened to the public. How lucky we are in Herefordshire lately! The picture on this page looks along a reed-fringed pool to a small boat moored. For me there is an air of mystery here: perhaps Ophelia is lying close by, or the Lady of Shallot is looking down from the stone tower which stands close to where I took this photograph.

I felt very excited about the image on the opposite page. The beautifully varied blues of the china pot so perfectly replicate the blues of the sunlit water, while the red geraniums give added fillip to the foreground and encourage us to explore further into the scene.

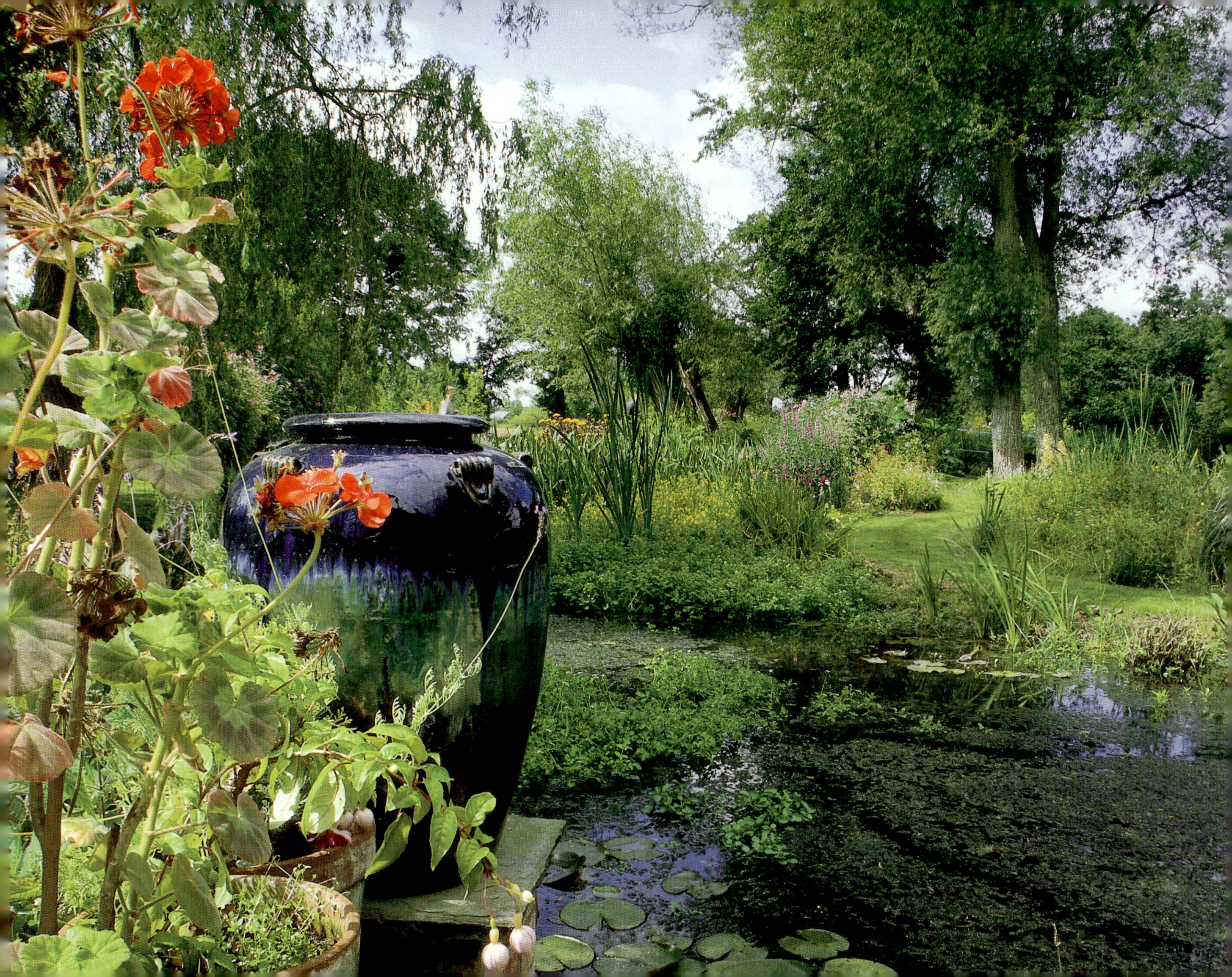

Going Down Hill on a Bicycle

Henry Charles Beeching

With lifted feet, hands still,
I am poised, and down the hill
Dart, with heedful mind;
The air goes by in a wind.

Swifter and yet more swift,
Till the heart with a mighty lift
Makes the lungs laugh, the throat cry: –
'O bird, see; see, bird, I fly.

'Is this, is this your joy?
O bird, then I, though a boy,
For a golden moment share
Your feathery life in air!'

Say, heart, is there aught like this
In a world that is full of bliss?
'Tis more than skating, bound
Steel-shod to the level ground.

Speed slackens now, I float
Awhile in my airy boat;
Till, when the wheels scarce crawl,
My feet to the treadles fall.

Alas, the longest hill
Must end in a vale; but still.
Who climbs with toil, wheresoe'er,
Shall find wings waiting there.

Left: Looking up to the spire of St Mary's, Ross-on-Wye.

Opposite page: The prospect west from Linton Hill across to Weston-under-Penyard and Penyard Park.

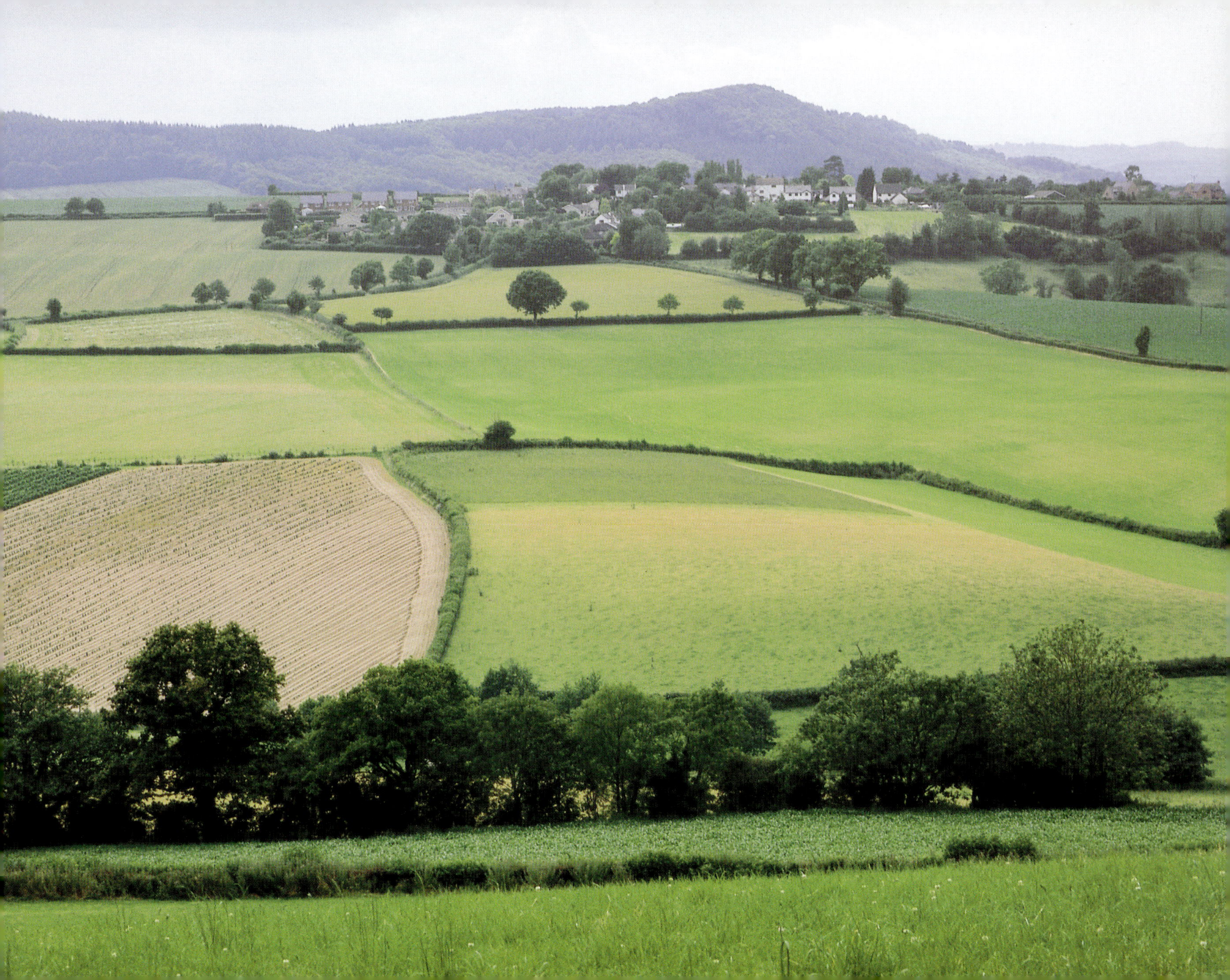

BOLLITREE CASTLE NEAR ROSS-ON-WYE

This was a journey back in time for me. I came here as a girl of fifteen to buy a redundant point-to-point mare of 15.2 hands. I remember she had produced a one-eyed foal, so perhaps the owners thought she might not be the best of breeding stock!

The trip down memory lane provided the delightful images reproduced here. The mid-eighteenth century Gothic wall and towers reflected in the green moat, and, across the road, the splendid gateways and rich old brick wall behind a false acacia tree.

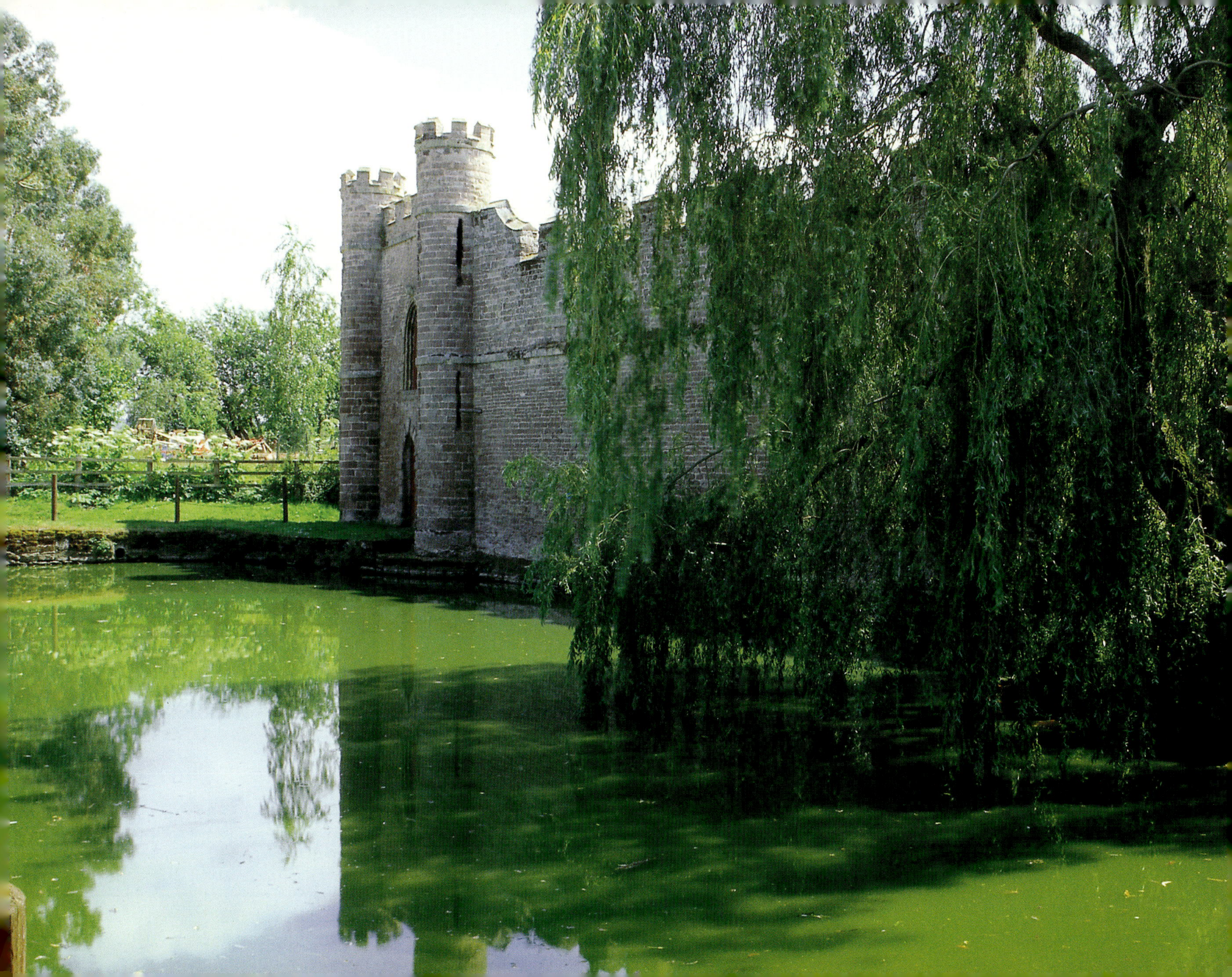

The Old Workman

Thomas Hardy

'Why are you so bent down before your time,
Old mason? Many have not left their prime
So far behind at your age, and can still
Stand full upright at will.'

He pointed to the mansion-front hard by,
And to the stones of the quoin against the sky;
'Those upper blocks,' he said, 'that there you see,
It was that ruined me.'

There stood in the air up to the parapet
Crowning the corner height, the stones as set
By him – ashlar whereon the gales might drum
For centuries to come.

'I carried them up,' he said, 'by a ladder there;
The last was as big a load as I could bear;
But on I heaved; and something in my back
Moved, as 'twere with a crack.

'So I got crookt. I never lost that sprain;
And those who live there, walled from wind and rain
By freestone that I lifted, do not know
That my life's ache came so.

'They don't know me, or even know my name,
But good I think it, somehow, all the same
To have kept 'em safe from harm, and right and tight,
Though it broke me quite.

'Yes; that I fixed it firm up there I am proud,
Facing the hail and snow and sun and cloud,
And to stand storms for ages, beating round
When I lie underground.'

Hampton Court
This classic English scene could have been taken at any time since the invention of photography. We are looking across the parkland to the south façade, remodelled by Wyatville for Richard Arkwright, and paid for out of Lancashire cotton-spinning money.

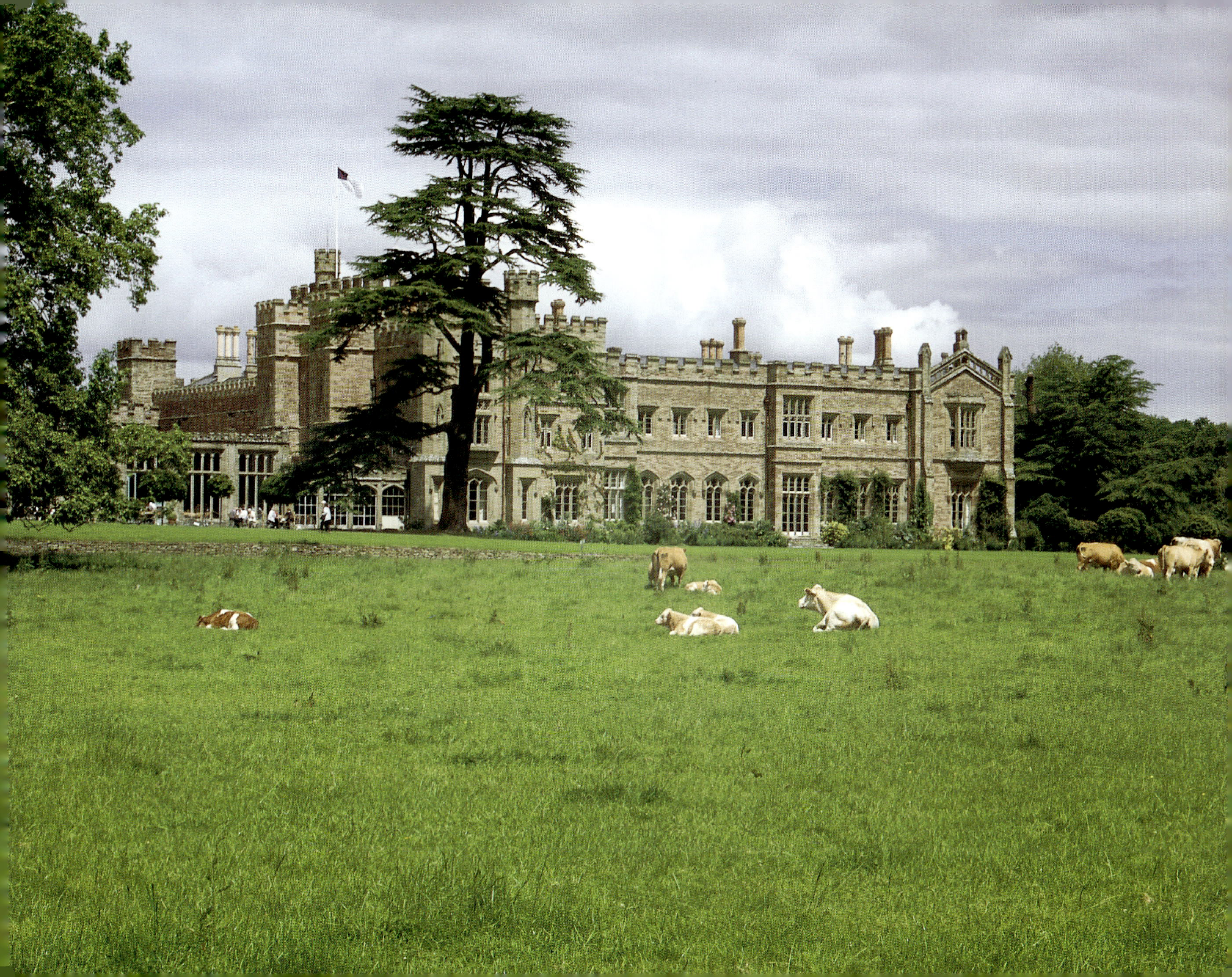

The Waggon-Maker

John Masefield

I have made tales in verse, but this man made
Waggons of elm to last a hundred years;
The blacksmith forged the rims and iron gears,
His was the magic that the wood obeyed.

Each deft device that country wisdom bade,
Or farmers' practice needed, he preserved.
He wrought the subtle contours, straight and curved,
Only by eye, and instinct of the trade.

No weakness, no offence in any part,
It stood the strain in mired fields and roads
In all a century's struggle for its bread;
Bearing, perhaps, eight thousand heavy loads.
Beautiful always as a work of art,
Homing the bride, and harvest, and men dead.

Leslie Evans in his Workshop at Eardisland

Leslie is a friend of more than thirty years: he produces fine garden and church furniture, and is one of England's most renowned and knowledgable bell-ringers. At the time of publishing this book he is aproaching his ninetieth birthday, still working daily and ringing three-hour peals.

His picture was chosen to accompany The Waggon-Maker poem because he works so much with wood, and because his father made waggons at Mansel Lacy.

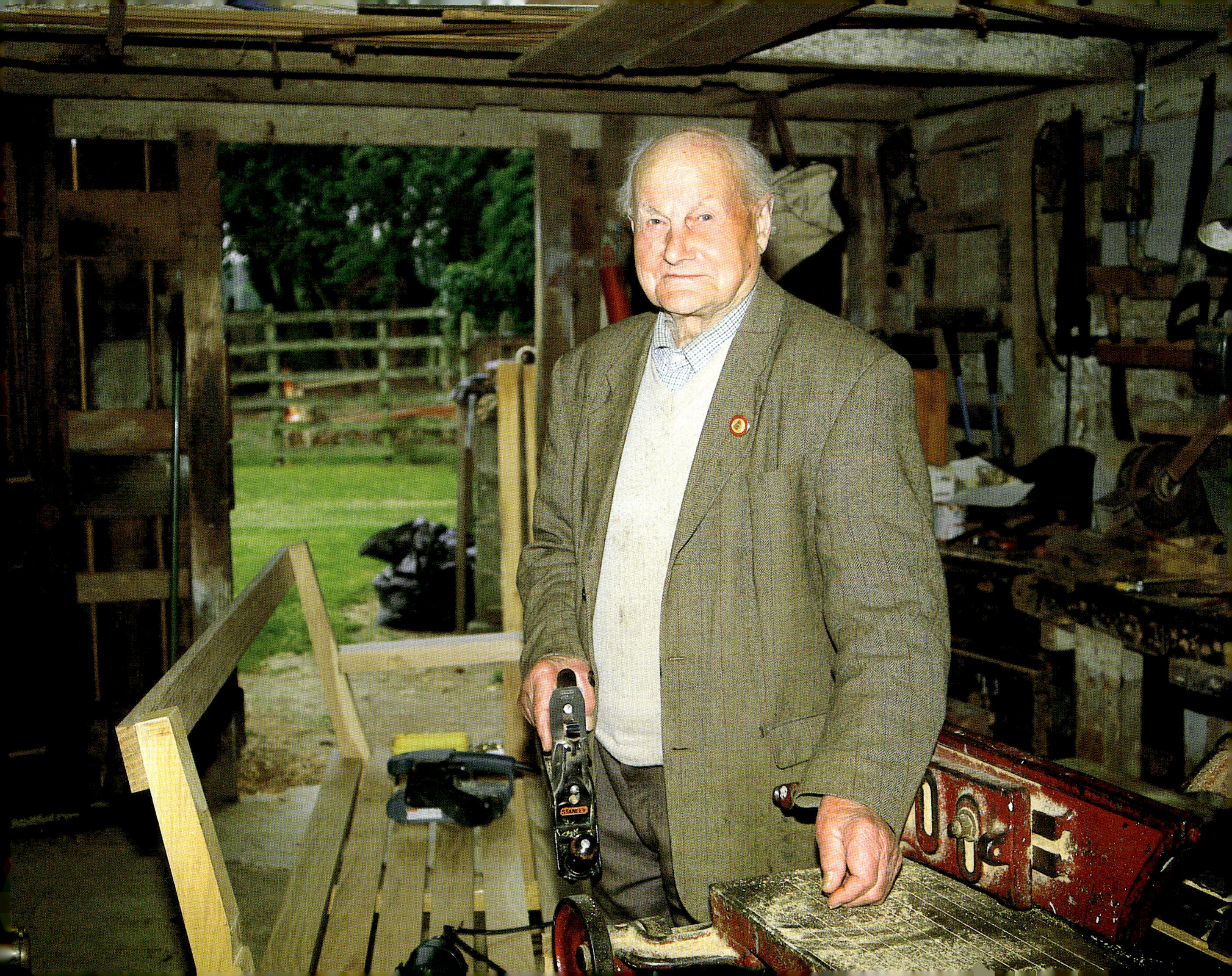
STANLEY

WE'LL GATHER LILACS ...

This scene, I thought, epitomised spring in England. I found its freshness particularly enjoyable when I was making my way down towards Goodrich church one spring morning.

from
To the Cuckoo

WILLIAM WORDSWORTH

O blithe New-comer! I have heard,
I hear thee and rejoice.
O Cuckoo! shall I call thee Bird,
Or but a wandering Voice?

While I am lying on the grass
Thy twofold shout I hear,
From hill to hill it seems to pass,
At once far off, and near.

Though babbling only to the Vale,
Of sunshine and of flowers,
Thou bringest unto me a tale
Of visionary hours.

Thrice welcome, darling of the Spring!
Even yet thou art to me
No bird, but an invisible thing,
A voice, a mystery.

HEREFORDSHIRE LANDSCAPES

This page: View towards The Knapp, Bredwardine. I know the area fairly well and always think the hillside with its small, artificial-looking tump has a rather dreamlike quality, reminiscent perhaps of a Marc Chagall painting.

Opposite page: Looking down into Hope Mansell Valley. The zig-zag hedge line leads us down into this delightful secret valley which is the inner ring of the geologically renowned Hope Mansell dome.

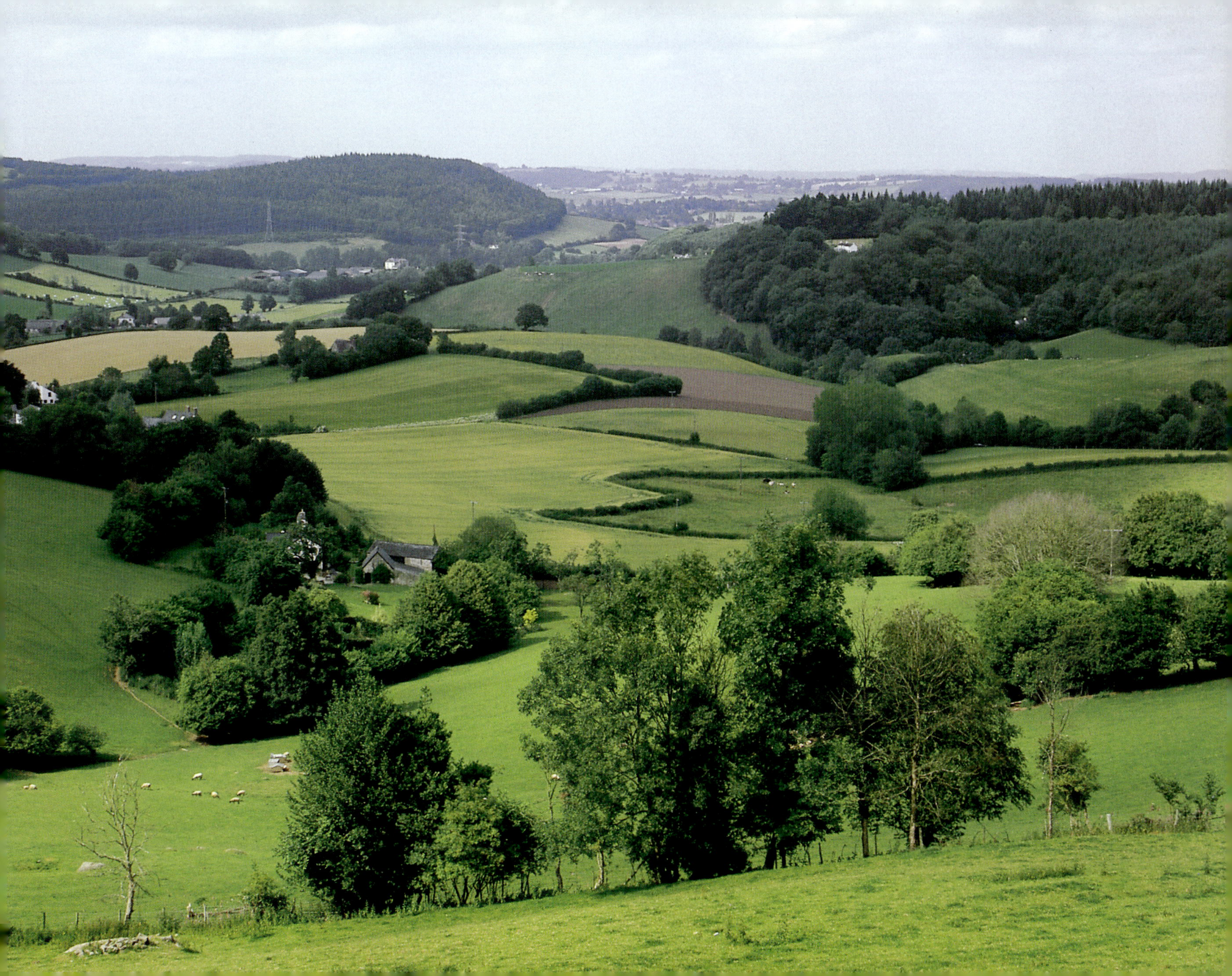

WHERE ENGLAND MERGES INTO WALES

This page: Looking west along the Monnow Valley. Before I took this photograph I talked to a man walking his dog, who was renting a nearby holiday cottage for the second successive year. He valued the tranquillity and the glorious sunrises through the bedroom window.

Opposite page: A Prospect towards Ysgyryd Fawr. The Monnow is down in the trees and we are looking out of Herefordshire towards the famous mountain slip visible across much of the county. Some say the slip took place on Good Friday, others that the Devil took a bite. My viewpoint is above Grove Farm, Walterstone where Christine Hunt runs the Cellar Gallery. Please see Index and Gazetteer under Cellar Gallery.

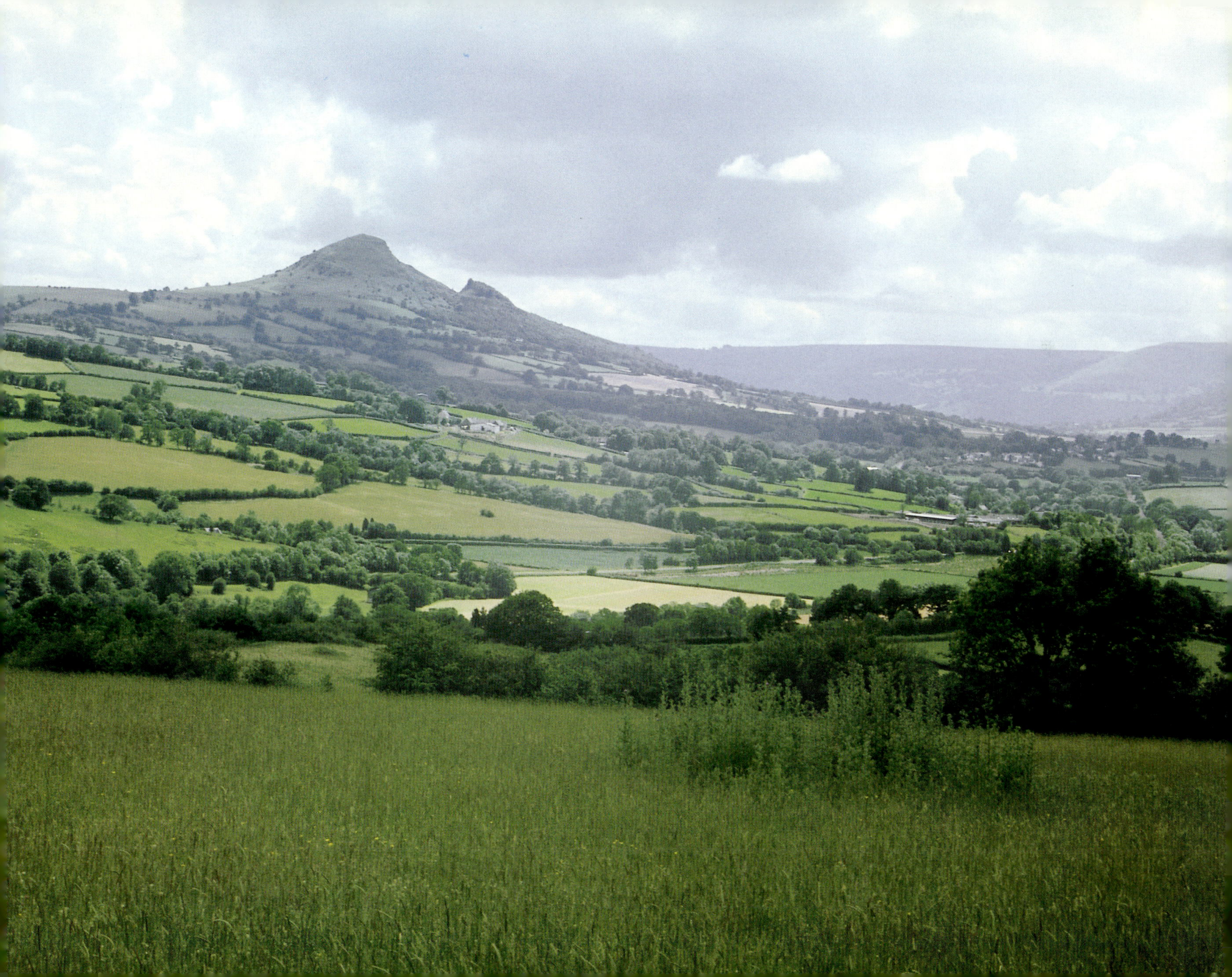

The River Monnow below Kentchurch

The Monnow is a beautiful river, especially on a sunny summer afternoon, when the sunlight is filtered through the trees onto the fast-flowing water. In this part of its course it forms the county boundary. I took these views from the Welsh bank. The little footbridge in the picture above must be one of the least used bridges linking England and Wales!

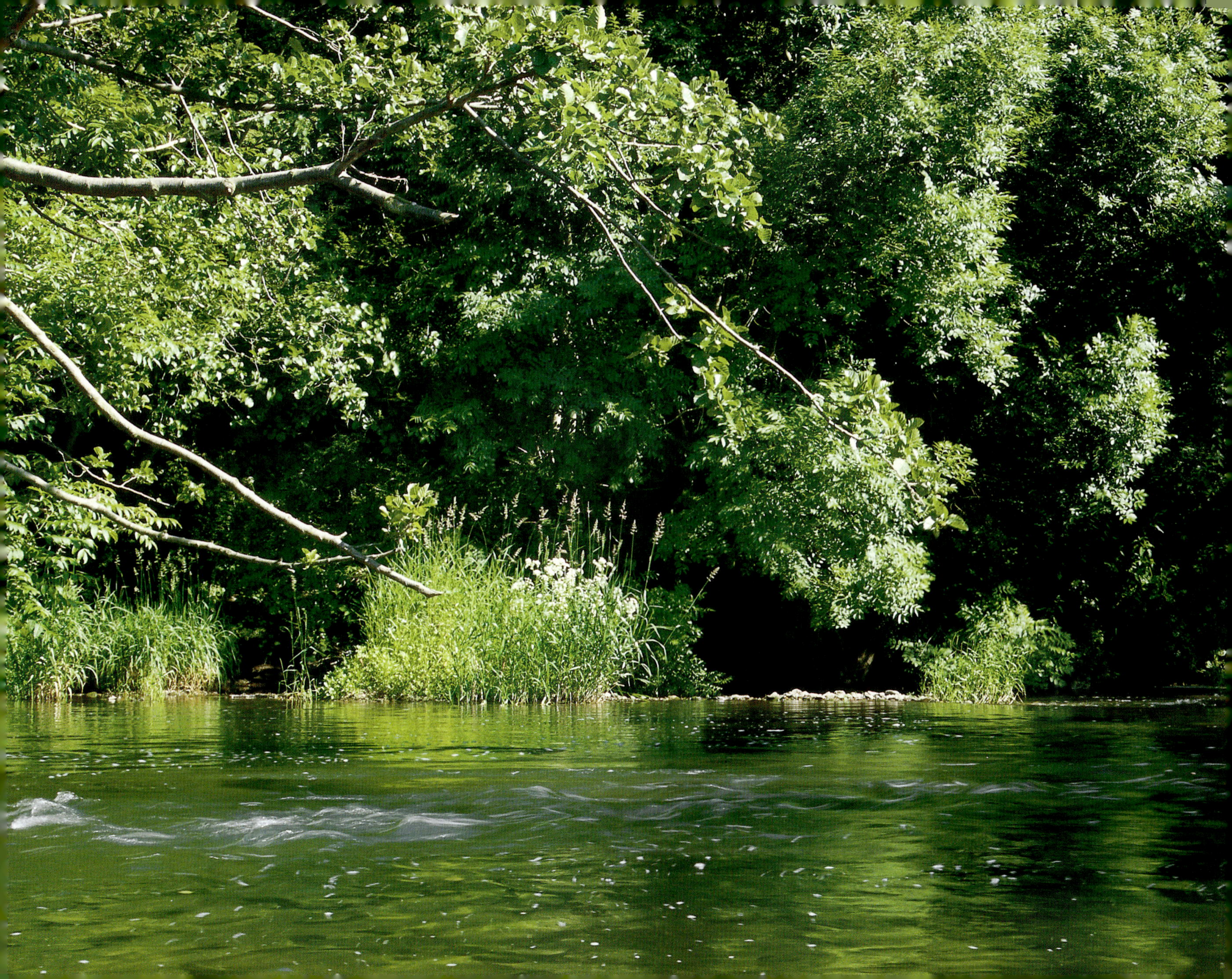

A Wish

Samuel Rogers

Mine be a cot beside the hill;
A beehive's hum shall soothe my ear;
A willowy brook that turns a mill,
With many a fall shall linger near.

The swallow, oft, beneath my thatch
Shall twitter from her clay-built nest;
Oft shall the pilgrim lift the latch,
And share my meal, a welcome guest.

Around my ivied porch shall spring
Each fragrant flower that drinks the dew;
And Lucy, at her wheel, shall sing
In russet-gown and apron blue.

The village church among the trees,
Where first our marriage vows were given,
With merry peals shall swell the breeze
And point with taper spire to heaven.

Timeless Herefordshire

Left: The cottage adjoining the now redundant watermill at Lower Burton, near Eardisland.

Opposite page: The prospect east from Garway Hill on a peaceful summer evening.

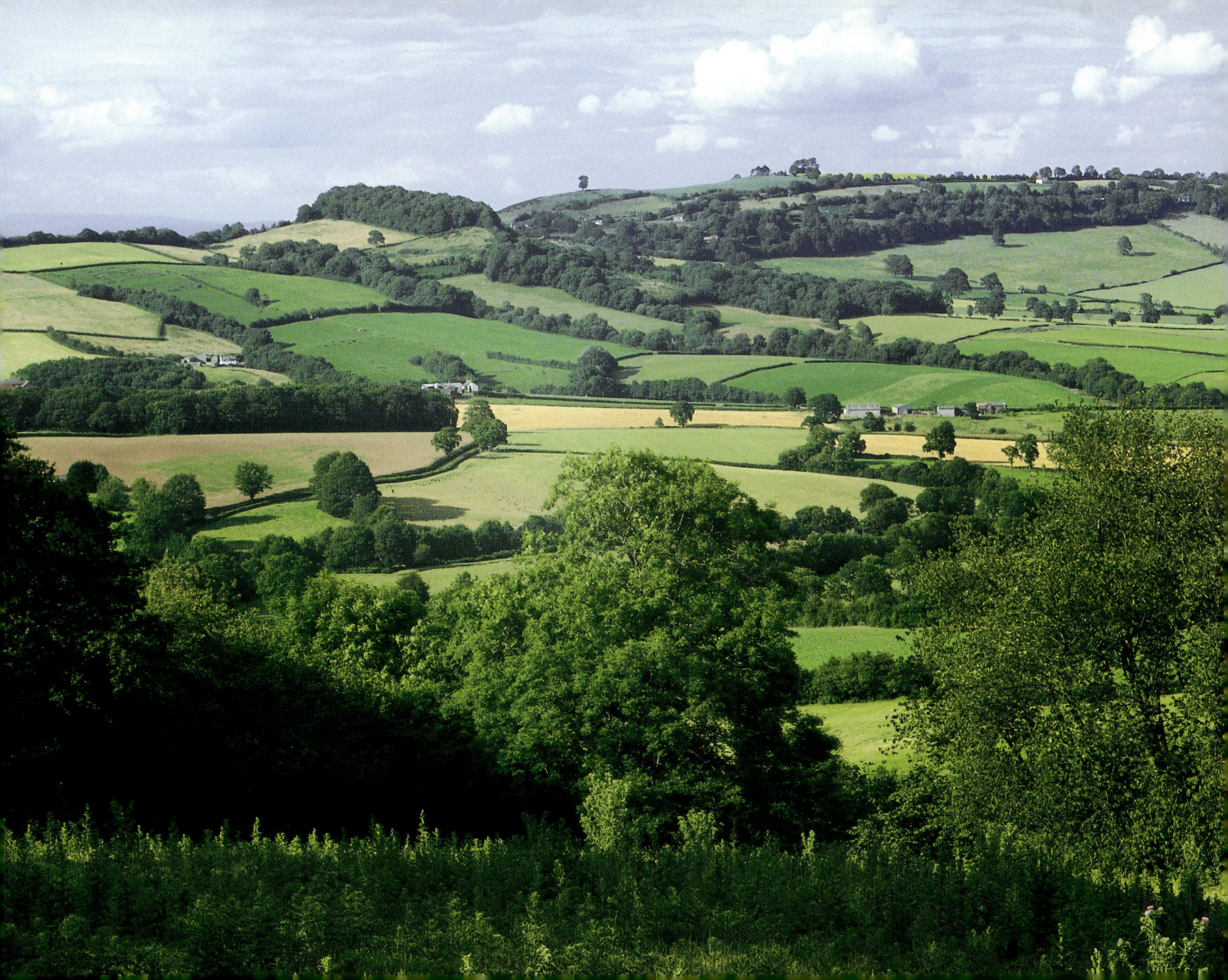

The Swallows
Andrew Young

All day – when early morning shone
With every dewdrop its own dawn
And when cockchafers were abroad
Hurtling like missiles that had lost their road.

The Swallows twisting here and there
Round unseen corners of the air
Upstream and down so quickly passed
I wondered that their shadows flew as fast.

They steeple-chased over the bridge
And dropped down to a drowning midge
Sharing the river with the fish,
Although the air itself was their chief dish.

Blue-winged snowballs! until they turned
And then with ruddy breasts they burned;
All in one instant everywhere,
Jugglers with their own bodies in the air.

Country Churches

Left: Kimbolton church is isolated from any houses in the parish but very well maintained. We see it here thrown into sharp relief by the setting sun.

Opposite page: Ocle Pychard features an unusual copper-covered broach spire, seen here in the morning sunlight.

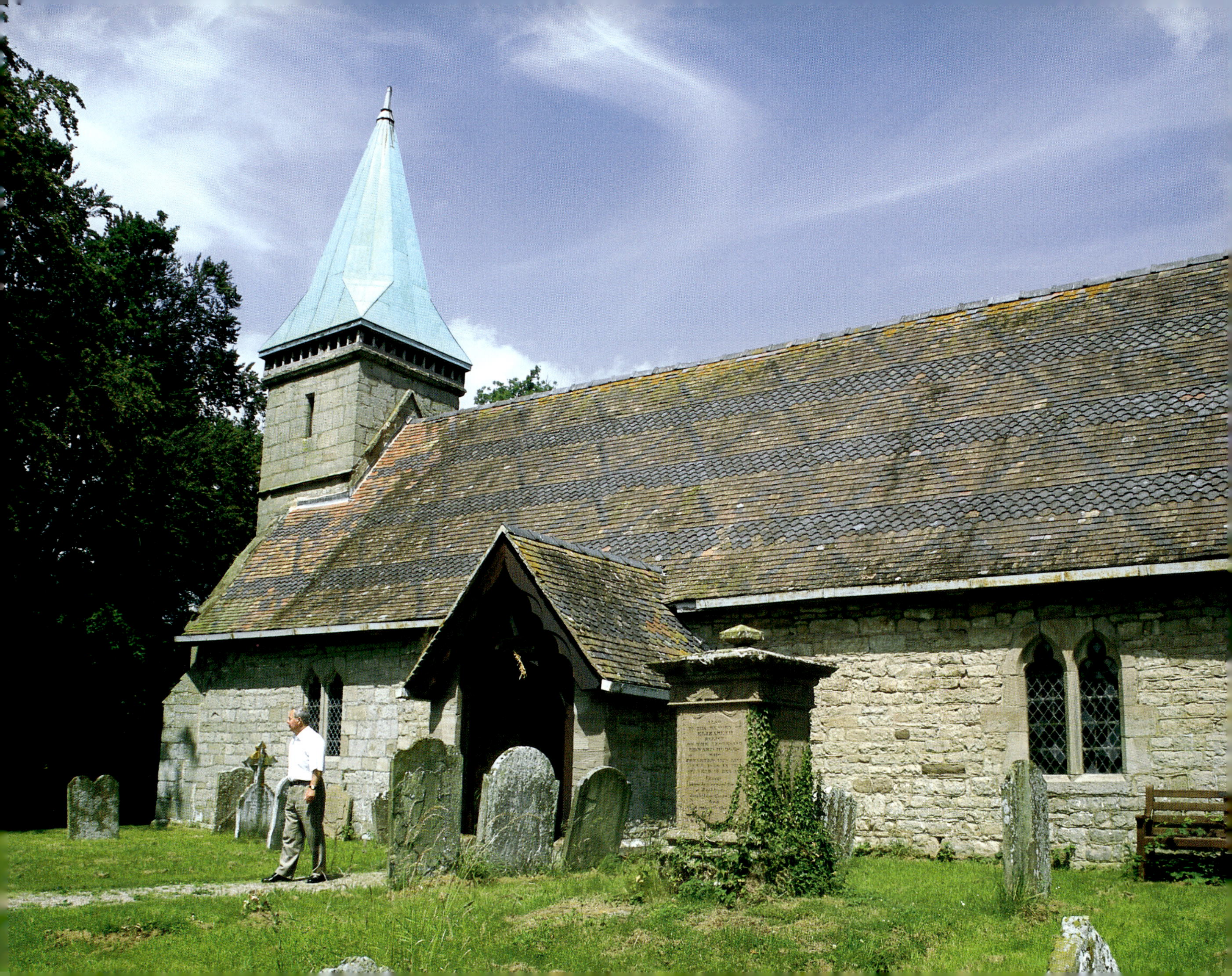

EVIDENCE OF PAST ERAS

Above: Titley Junction. The owners kindly let me photograph the admirably preserved country station. I was fascinated by the myriad wild strawberry plants flowering profusely between the railway lines. Perhaps they seeded there when the railway was functioning.

Opposite page: St Michael's church stands well above its village at Lyonshall. A tramway ran along the base of the wall in the foreground; an old house across the road is still called The Wharf. The castle ruins are in the trees behind the chancel, and a clear section of Offa's Dyke is just west of the church.

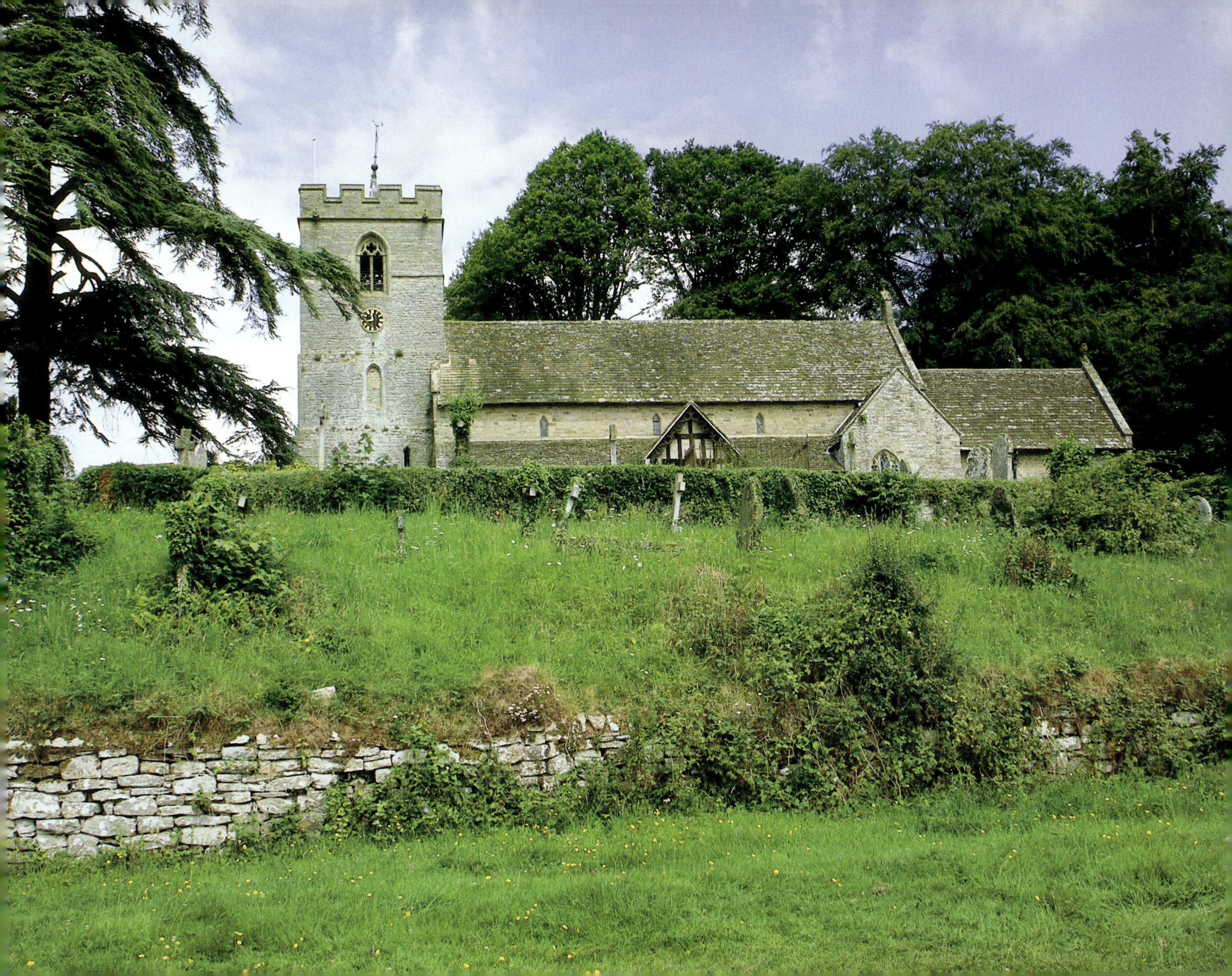

Hergest Croft Gardens

I have made so many visits to this wonderful place through the years and will never tire of it: the wonderful azaleas, rhododendrons and hundreds of specimen trees make it one of Britain's special and unique places.

One can spend hours here at almost any time of the year, for there are not only the formal gardens, and the shrubberies and arboretum, but the hidden delights of Park Wood.

The Banks family have been prominent in the plant collecting world for several generations; in Park Wood, in a deep ravine they have recreated, as nearly as possible on the Welsh border, a Himalayan valley which blazes with colour in late spring and early summer.

In the picture on the opposite page the long shadows across the lawn indicate the majestic height of the trees to the left of the picture. Overleaf, on page 71, is just an indication of the wonderful array of colour that awaits visitors each year.

Please see details in the Index and Gazetteer

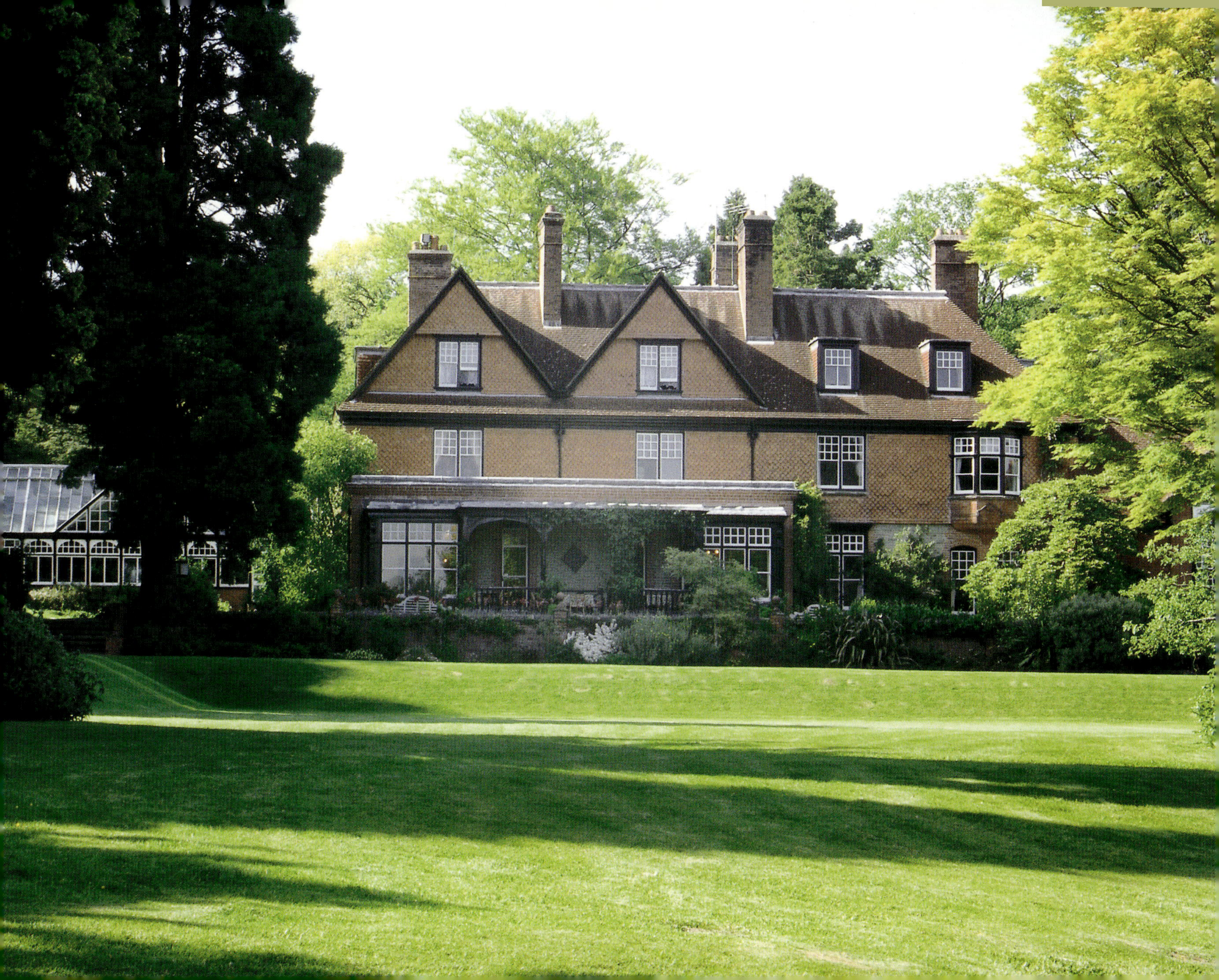

Hedgehog

Anthony Thwaite

Twitching the leaves just where the drainpipe clogs
In ivy leaves and mud, a purposeful
Creature at night about its business. Dogs
Fear his stiff seriousness. He chews away

At beetles, worms, slugs, frogs. Can kill a hen
With one snap of his jaws, can taunt a snake
To death on muscled spines. Old countrymen
Tell tales of hedgehogs sucking a cow dry.

But this one, cramped by houses, fences, walls,
Must have slept here all winter in that heap
Of compost, or have inched by intervals
Through tidy gardens to this ivy bed.

And here, dim-eyed, but ears so sensitive
A voice within the house can make him freeze.
He scuffs the edge of danger; yet can live
Happily in our nights and absences.

A country creature, wary, quiet and shrewd,
He takes the milk we give him, when we're gone.
At night, our slamming voices must seem crude
To one who sits and waits for silences.

HEDGEHOG SIESTA TIME

It's not easy to find a picture to illustrate a poem on hedgehogs. This one was curled up in some straw at Barton Hill Animal Centre, Kentchurch.

Opposite page: In Hergest Croft Gardens.

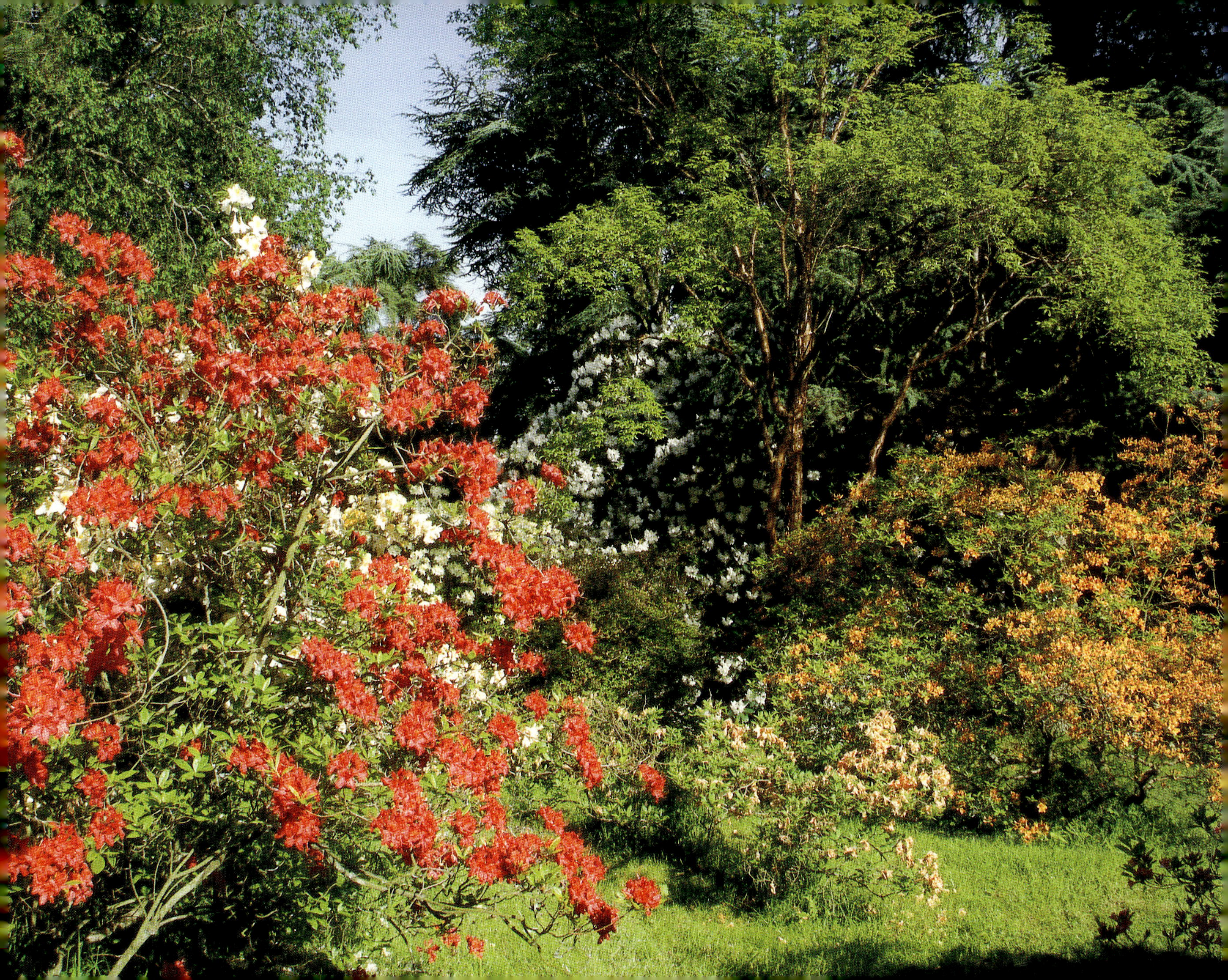

The Return
L. A. G. STRONG

The village church, so small it has hardly shrunk
Since I, a child, unlatched the heavy door
And tiptoed in; the pulpit, like the trunk
Of a squat thick tree; the screen that Cromwell tore
And hacked, and grieving pious hands renewed;
And. measuring the silence, the old clock,
Fifty years shrivel to an interlude;
No change; porch, pulpit, screen, and strong tick-tock
Whittling my visit from the calendar,
With stern, sharp stroke cancelling every breath;
And I am still that small parishioner
Who recognized the beat of life and death,
Pondered and nodded, looked up unafraid –
Then, flooded with foreknowledge, knelt and prayed.

Opposite page
All over Herefordshire one encounters little parish churches beautifully maintained by scattered communities. Here is another example at Evesbatch, encountered on a sunny afternoon exploring the Leadon and Frome valleys along the north-eastern edge of the county.

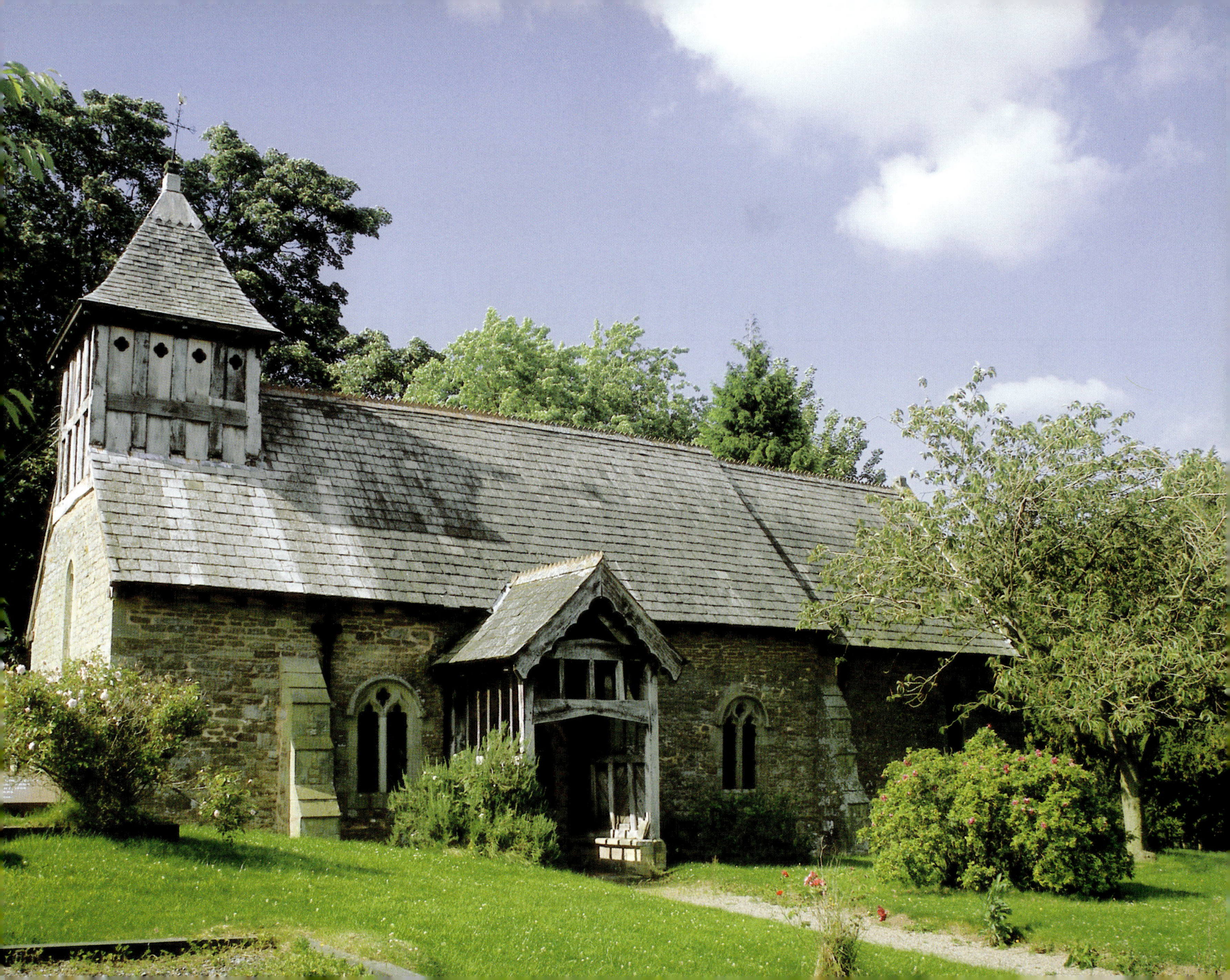

AN EVENING IN LEOMINSTER

The great glory of Leominster Priory is the west front, and I knew it could only be satisfactorily photographed when the sun was high in the west; hence a special trip on a June evening to take this picture.

I took numerous shots from a variety of angles, selecting the one on the opposite page where the greenery framed the building, masking the deep shadow on the south side and adding a touch of colour. The sky, a deep Mediterranean azure, provided the perfect background for the tower.

I was glad I went on to nearby Grange Court. The sun was illuminating the heavily-timbered front in patches of light, adding an extra black and white pattern to a much photographed façade, and obscuring the rather incongruous conservatory in deep shadow.

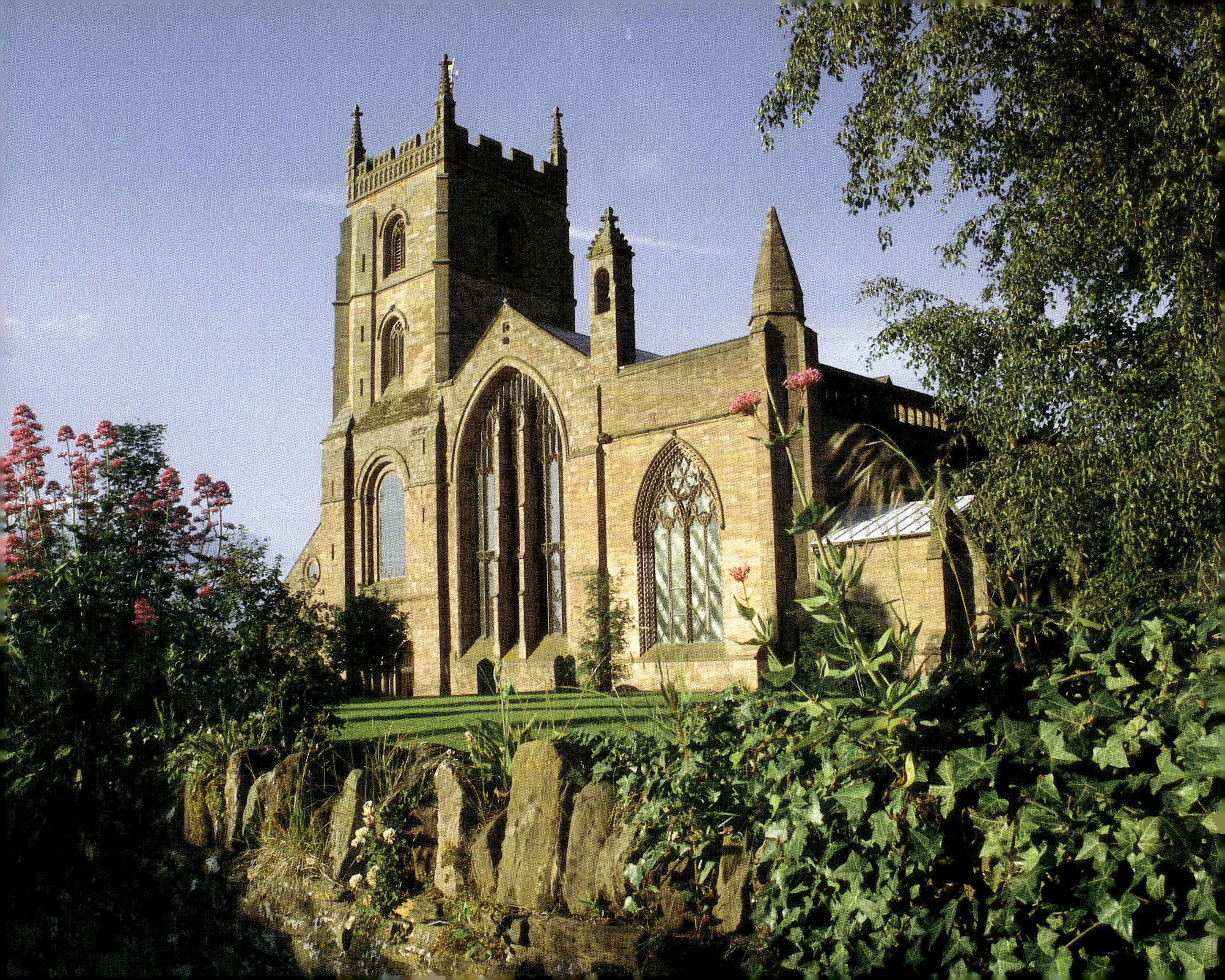

from The Barn
Stephen Spender

Half hidden by trees, the sheer roof of the barn
Is a river of tiles, warped
By winding currents of weather
Suns and storms ago.

Through beech leaves, its vermilion seems
A Red Admiral's wing, with veins
Of lichen and rust, an underwing
Of winter-left leaves.

Now, in the Spring, a sapling's jet
Of new, pure flame, cuts across
The low long gutter. One leaf holds up
Red tiles reflected in its cup.

A ghost of a noise—the hint of a gust
Caught in the rafter centuries ago:
The creak of a winch, the wood turn of a wheel.

A Memorable Stop at Rowlestone

It's the chance encounters in unexpected places that make my excursions so memorable. Rowlestone is just two houses, a church, and a barn at a little crossroads, and it was the barn that immediately fascinated me.

The barn was derelict and I needed to get in close for the shot I wanted. Climbing the gate I set off towards it only to sink ankle deep in what looked like firm ground, but wet and muddy canvas shoes are a minor price to pay for the photograph one is determined to have!

I found myself mesmerised by the timelessness of the building. Swallows were darting in and out of small holes in the wall: other larger holes had obviously been used to encourage owls to take up residence in the times when they were the most effective pest control. The barn was completely unaltered, and I could have been in Constable's England.

When I returned to the car with the evidence of my trespassing all over my squelching shoes, I encountered a very pleasant lady who was the owner of the barn. To my amazement she guessed who I was. She told me that her daughter had planning permission to convert it into a house.

It is splendid that redundant buildings can be given a new lease of life, and it will make a lovely house … but I'm glad I went to Rowlestone in time to capture it before it changes for ever.

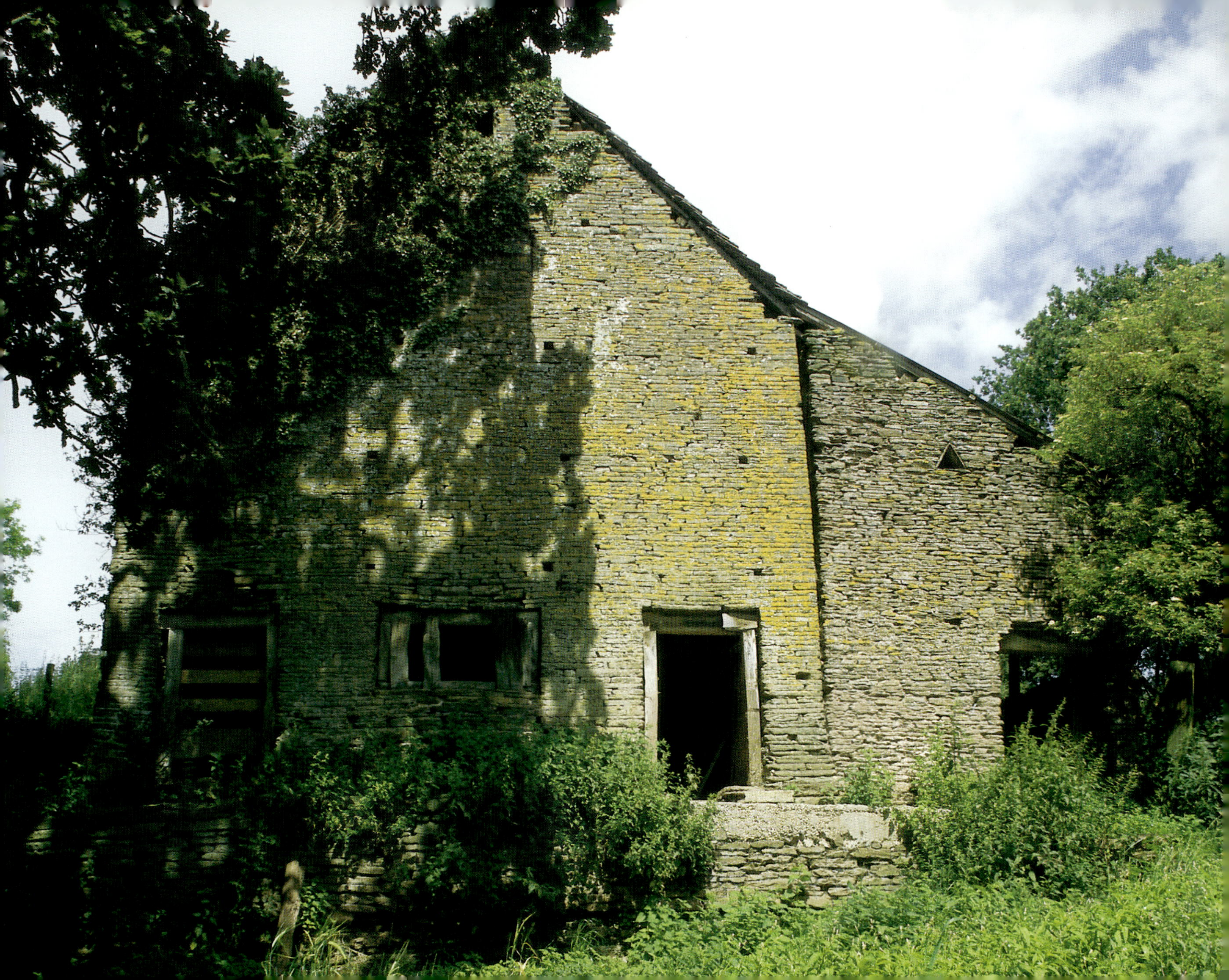

The Vacant Farmhouse
Walter de la Mare

Three gables; clustered chimney stacks; a wall
Snowed every Spring with cherry, gage, and pear,
Now suckered, rank, unpruned. Green-seeded, tall,
A drift of sullen nettles souring near—
Beside a staved-in stye and green-scummed pond,
Where once duck-dabbled sunshine rippled round.

Dark empty barns; a shed; abandoned byres;
A weedy stack-yard whence all life has fled;
A derelict wain, with loose and rusted tyres;
And an enormous elm-tree overhead …

That attic casement … Was there flaw in the glass? …
I thought, as I glanced up, there had peered a face.
But no. Still: eyes are strange; for at my steady stare
Through the cool sunlit evening air,
Scared silent sparrows flew up out of the ivy there
Into an elder tree—for perching place.

ANOTHER CHANCE ENCOUNTER

"We need a ruined farmhouse," Barry said, and a few days later there it was, the perfect example, stark and alone in a field overlooking the Frome Valley. Sometimes you can hardly believe your luck!

Fortunately the car could be backed into a field, and off I trudged as ever to get the right setting for the latest find. In the end, however, I selected this fairly long shot, framed by the tree to give a sense of place. I like the simple hard edges of the building silhouetted on the skyline and holding out against the elements on its exposed west-facing hillside.

But the building and I were not completely alone. To the left of the tree you can just make out the crow I startled taking off, protesting noisily.

Another chance encounter … another memorable picture.

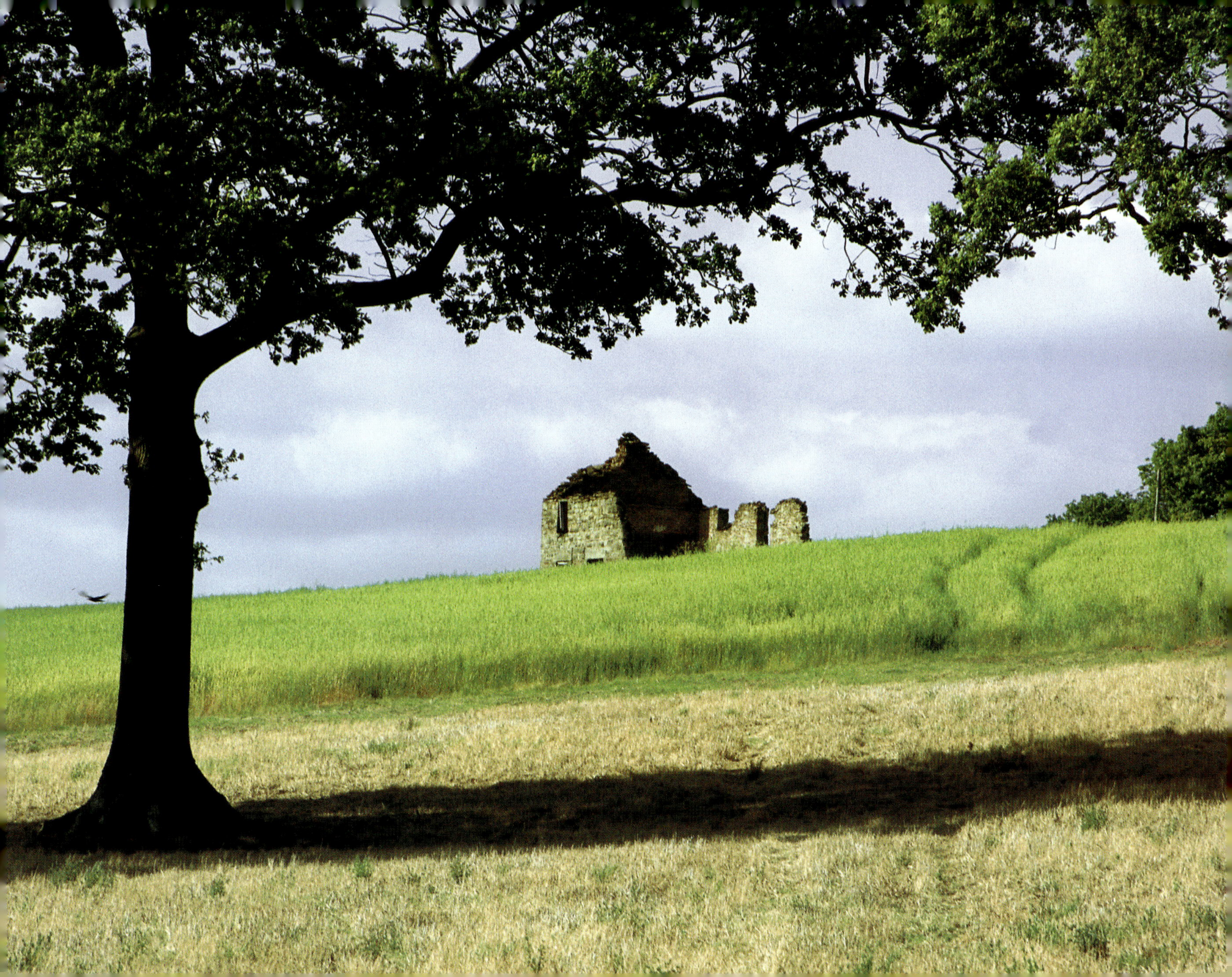

Duty

Ellen S. Hooper

I slept and dreamed that life was Beauty:
I woke and found that life was Duty:
Was then the dream a shadowy lie?
Toil on, sad heart, courageously,
And thou shalt find thy dream to be
A noonday light and truth to thee.

Left: The chapel at Dinmore Manor is 14th-century, and dedicated to the Knights of St John of Jerusalem. In contrast, the church at Dulas is of 1865, and looks more like a village school than a church. At Dulas we are in southwest Herefordshire, more Welsh than English in its landscape and place names. To create this picture I set the tripod low down on the road to provide a front framework of the meadowsweet growing along the churchyard wall.

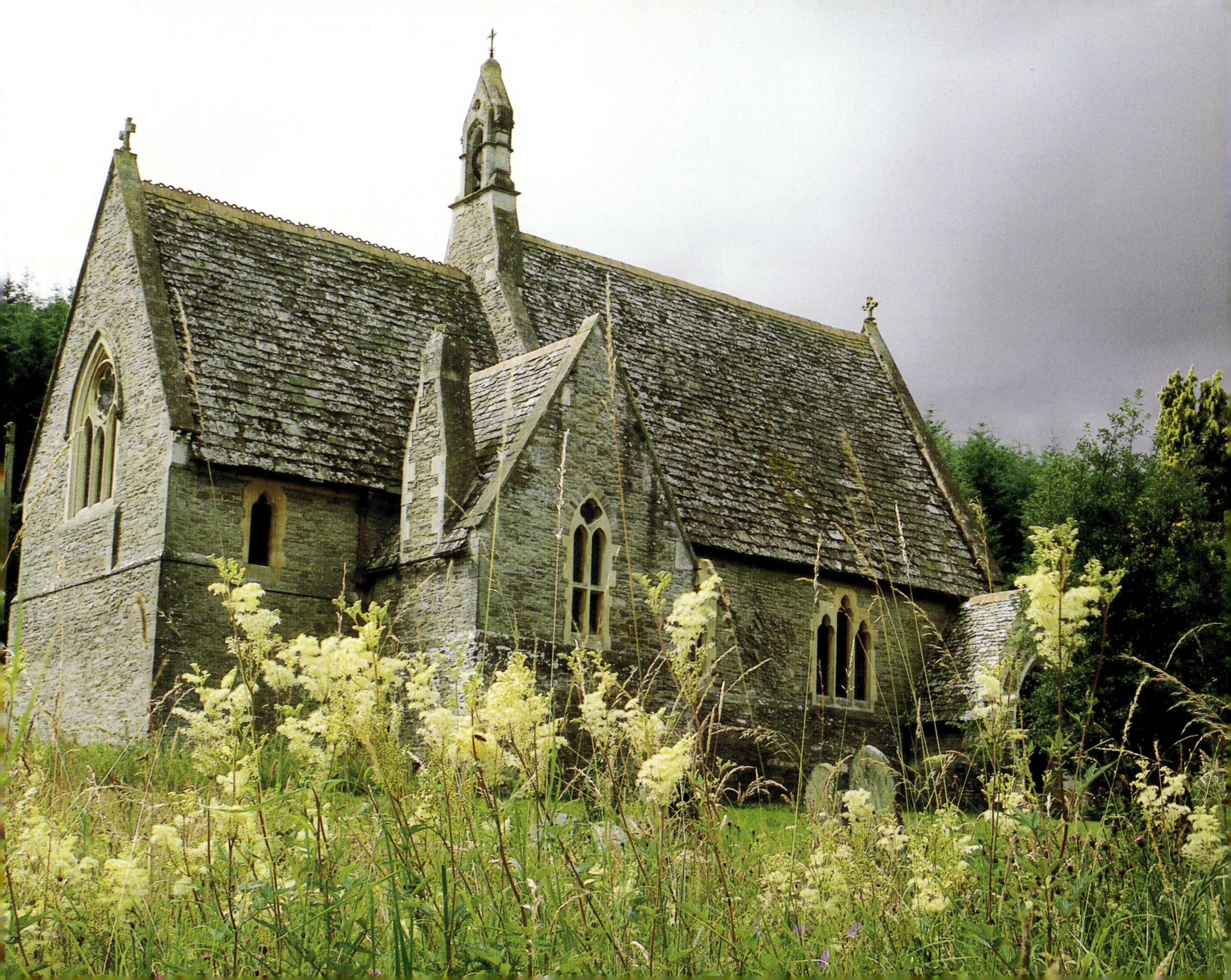

Roundabouts and Swings
Patrick R Chalmers

It was early last September nigh to Framlin'am-on-Sea,
An' 'twas Fair-day come to-morrow, an' the time was after tea.
An' I met a painted caravan adown a dusty lane,
A Pharaoh with his waggons comin' jolt an' creak an' strain;
A cheery cove an' sunburnt, bolt o' eye and wrinkled up.
An' beside him on the splashboard sat a brindled terrier pup,
An' a lurcher wise as Solomon an' lean as fiddle-strings
Was joggin' in the dust along 'is roundabouts and swings.

'Goo'-day,' said 'e: 'Goo'-day,' said I: 'an' 'ow d'you find things go,
An' what's the chance o' millions when you runs a travellin' show?'
"I find,' said 'e, 'things very much as 'ow I've always found,
For mostly they goes up and down or else goes round and round.'
Said 'e, 'The job's the very spit o' what it always were,
It's bread and bacon mostly when the dog
    don't catch a 'are:
But lookin' at it broad, an' while it ain't no
    merchant king's,
What's lost upon the roundabouts we
    pulls up on the swings!'

'Goo' luck,' said 'e: 'Goo' luck,' said I: 'you've put it past a doubt:
An' keep that lurcher on the road, the gamekeepers is out':
'E thumped upon the footboard an' 'e lumbered on again
To meet a gold-dust sunset down the owl-light in the lane:
An' the moon she climbed the 'azels, while a nightjar seemed to spin
That Pharaoh's wisdom o'er again, 'is sooth of lose-and-win:
For 'up an' down an' round,' said 'e, 'goes all appointed things,
An' losses on the roundabouts means profits on the swings!'

BROMYARD GALA

From quite modest beginnings in 1967, Bromyard Gala has grown into one of the premier annual outdoor events of the West Midlands, combining an exciting mixture of traditional country show with steam engines and vintage and classic vehicles.

   I am always attracted to the great traction engines, with their gleaming twisted brasswork and lovingly oiled machinery. For the main picture I chose a shot from the entrance which I hope conveys the liveliness, the sights, the sounds, and the sense of excitement which makes these shows so perennially popular.

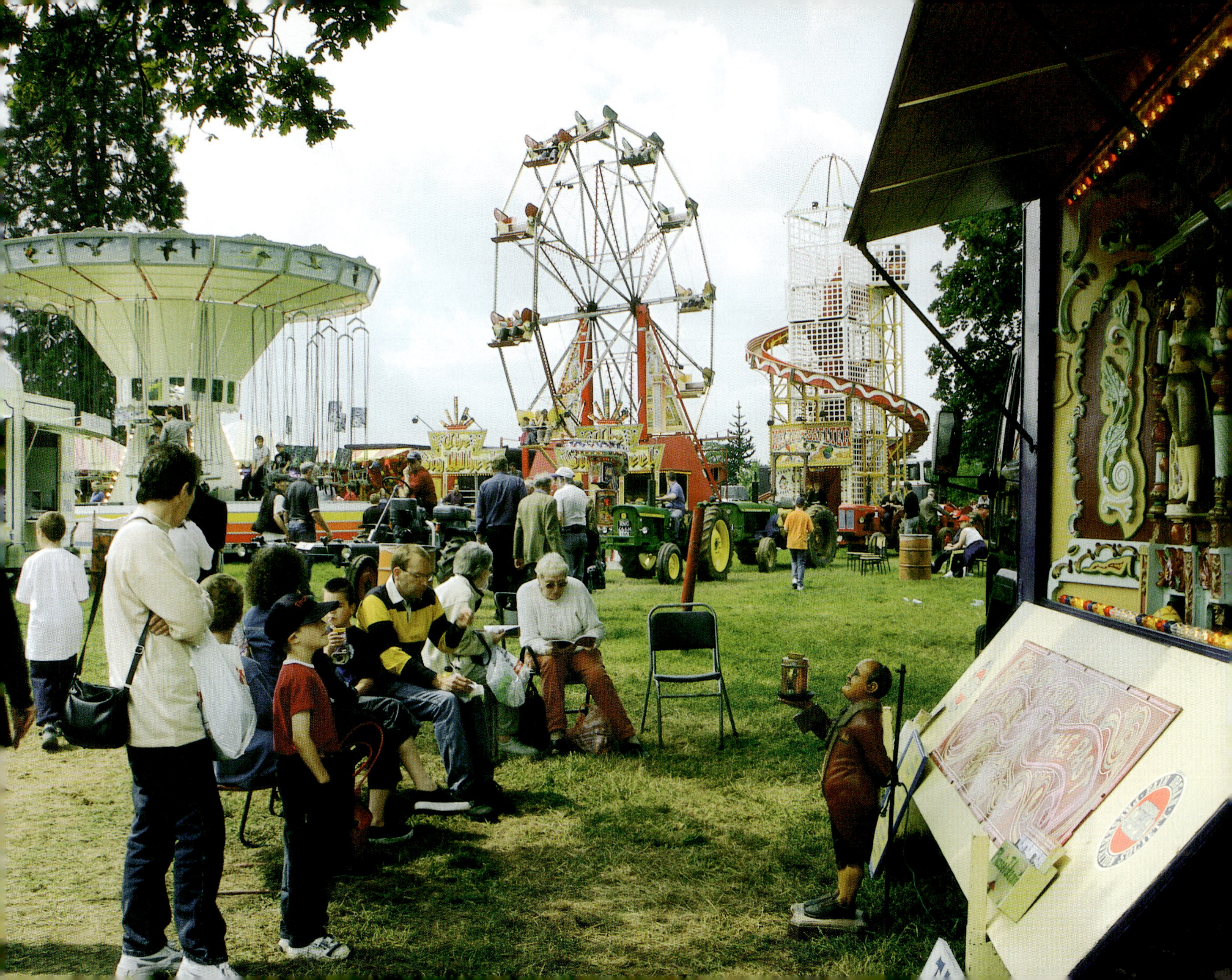

The Rolling English Road

G. K. Chesterton

Before the Roman came to Rye or out to Severn strode,
The rolling English drunkard made the rolling English road.
A reeling road, a rolling road, that rambles round the shire,
And after him the parson ran, the sexton and the squire;
A merry road, a mazy road, and such as we did tread
The night we went to Birmingham by way of Beachy Head.

I knew no harm of Bonaparte and plenty of the Squire,
And for to fight the Frenchman I did not much desire;
But I did bash their baggonets because they came arrayed
To straighten out the crooked road an English drunkard made,
Where you and I went down the lane with ale-mugs in our hands,
The night we went to Glastonbury by way of Goodwin Sands.

His sins they were forgiven him; or why do flowers run
Behind him; and the hedges all strengthening in the sun?
The wild thing went from left to right and knew not which was which,
But the wild rose was above him when they found him in the ditch.
God pardon us, nor harden us; we did not see so clear
The night we went to Bannockburn by way of Brighton Pier.

My friends, we will not go again or ape an ancient rage,
Or stretch the folly of our youth to be the shame of age,
But walk, with clearer eyes and ears this path that wandereth,
And see undrugged in evening light the decent inn of death;
For there is good news yet to hear and fine things to be seen
Before we go to Paradise by way of Kensal Green.

Prospect East from Linton Hill
Here we are looking across Gorsley Common into Gloucestershire, led into the scene by a typically meandering 'rolling English road'.

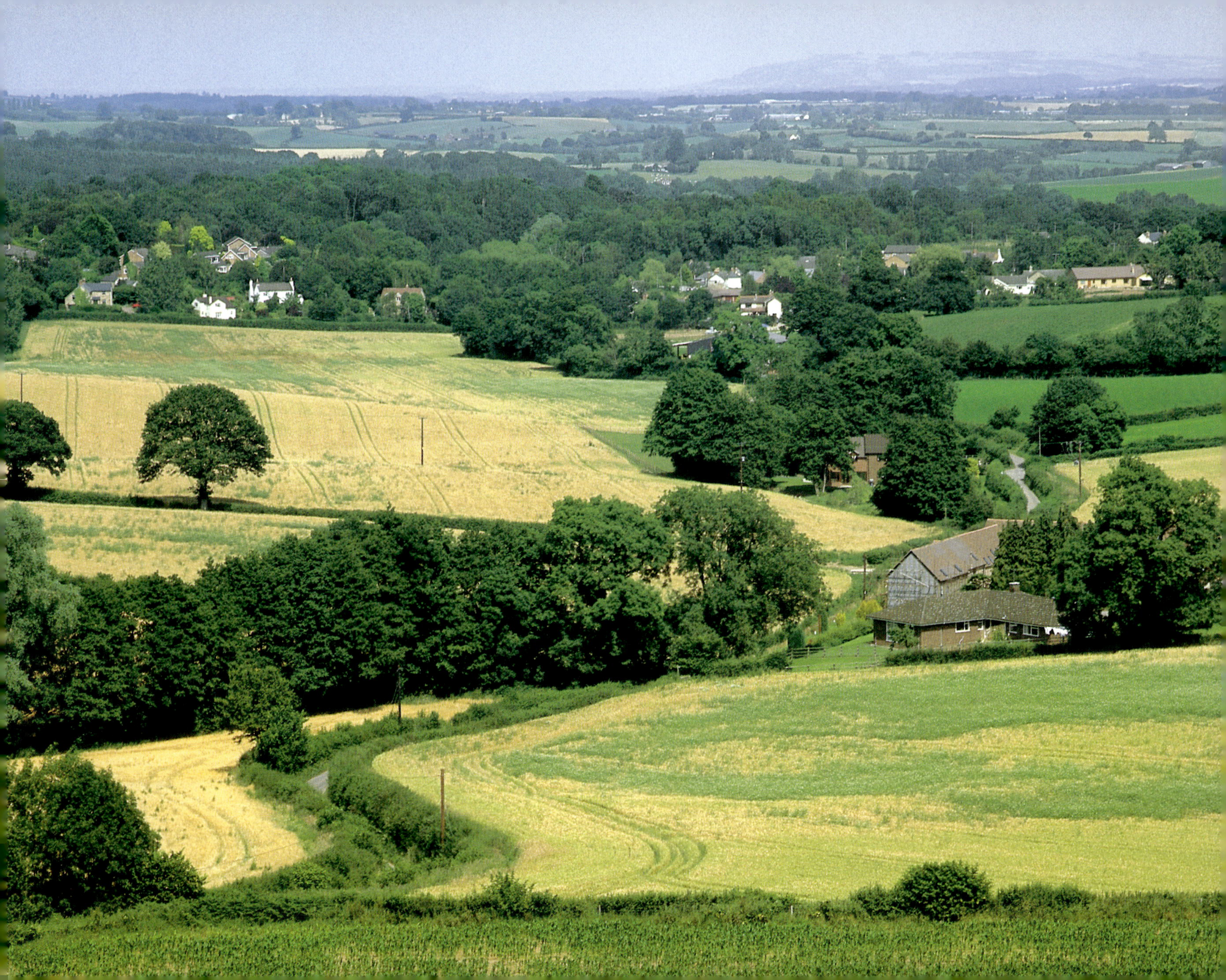

Morning

JOHN CLARE

The morning comes, the drops of dew
Hang on the grass and bushes too;
The sheep more eager bite the grass
Whose moisture gleams like drops of glass;
The heifer licks in grass and dew
That make her drink and fodder too.
The little bird his morn-song gives,
His breast wet with the dripping leaves.
Then stops abruptly just to fly
And catch the wakened butterfly,
That goes to sleep behind the flowers
Or backs of leaves from dews and showers.
The yellow-hammer, haply blest,
Sits by the dyke upon her nest;
The long grass hides her from the day,
The water keeps the boys away.
The morning sun is round and red
As crimson curtains round a bed.
The dewdrops hang on barley horns
As beads the necklace thread adorns,
The dewdrops hang wheat-ears upon
Like golden drops against the sun.
Hedge-sparrows in the bush cry 'tweet',
O'er nests larks winnow in the wheat,
Till the sun turns gold and gets more high,
And paths are clean and grass gets dry,
And longest shadows pass away.
And brightness is the blaze of day.

Morning at Bodenham Lake
Taken from the hide in the nature reserve.

Above: Horses on a cold, frosty morning.

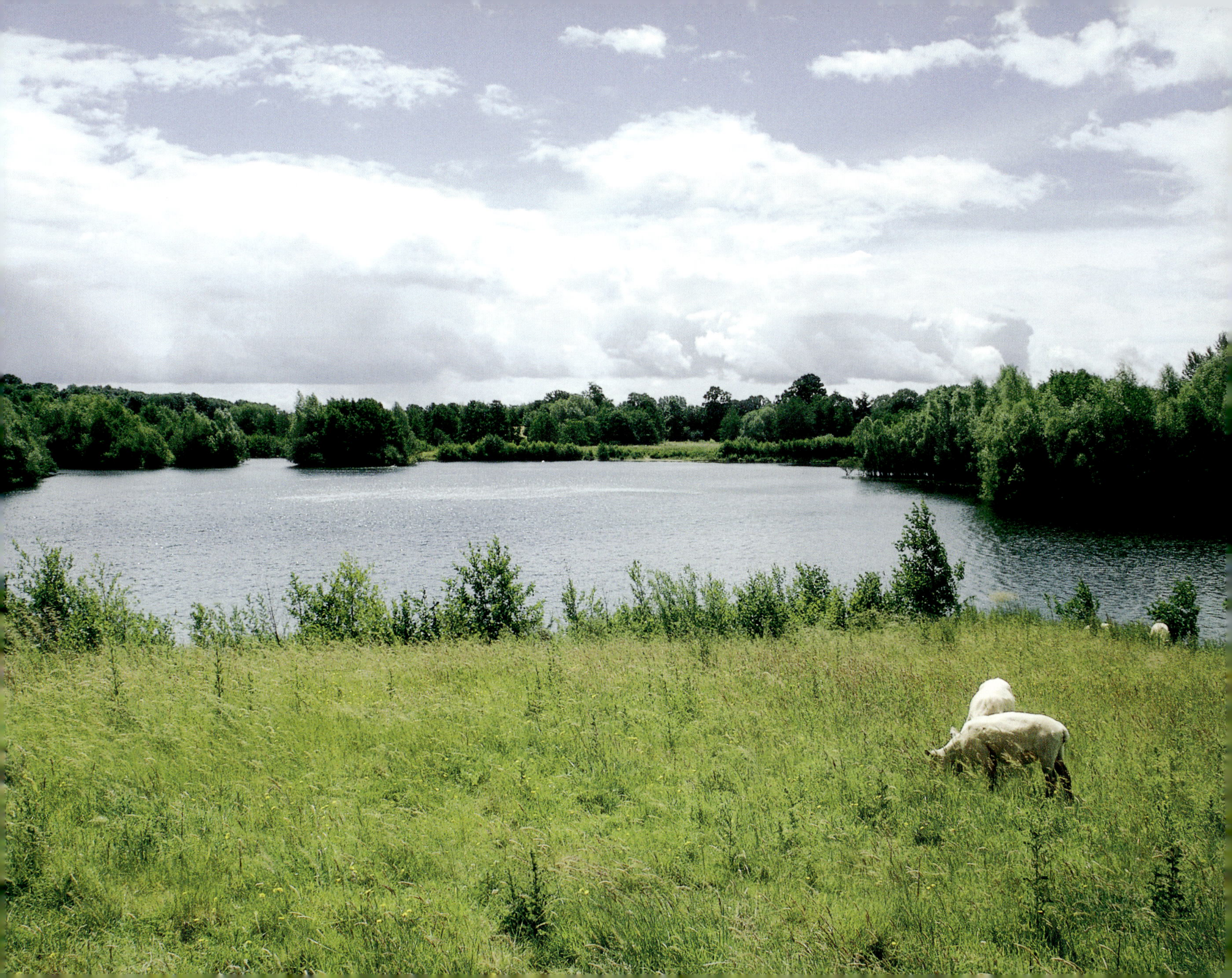

from The Brook

Alfred, Lord Tennyson

I come from haunts of coot and hern.
I make a sudden sally
And sparkle out among the fern,
Then bicker down a valley.

By thirty hills I hurry down,
Or slip between the ridges.
By twenty thorps, a little town,
And half a hundred bridges.

Till last by Philip's farm I flow
To join the brimming river.
For men may come and men may go,
But I go on for ever.

I chatter over stony ways,
In little sharps and trebles,
I bubble into eddying bays,
I babble on the pebbles.

With many a curve my banks I fret
By many a field and fallow,
And many a fairy foreland set
With willow-weed and mallow.

I chatter, chatter, as I flow
To join the brimming river,
For men may come and men may go,
But I go on for ever.

Above: A wary resident who prefers photographers not to intrude on his territory, and, far right, the infant River Frome downstream from Bishops Frome.

I wind about, and in and out,
With here a blossom sailing,
And here and there a lusty trout,
And here and there a grayling.

And here and there a foamy flake
Upon me, as I travel
With many a silvery waterbreak
Above the golden gravel.

And draw them all along, and flow
To join the brimming river,
For men may come and men may go,
But I go on for ever.I steal by lawns and grassy plots,
I slide by hazel covers;
I move the sweet forget-me-nots
That grow for happy lovers.

I slip. I slide. I gloom. I glance.
Among my skimming swallows:
I make the netted sunbeam dance
Against my sandy shallows.

I murmur under moon and stars
In brambly wildernesses:
I linger by my shingly bars:
I loiter round my cresses:

And out again I curve and flow
To join the brimming river.
For men may come and men may go,
But I go on for ever.

A Garden Song

Henry Austin Dobson

Here, in this sequestered close,
Bloom the hyacinth and rose;
Here beside the modest stock
Flaunts the flaring hollyhock;
Here, without a pang, one sees
Ranks, conditions, and degrees.

All the seasons run their race
In this quiet resting place;
Peach, and apricot, and fig
Here will ripen, and grow big.
Here is store and overplus, –
More had not Alcinous!

Here, in alleys cool and green,
Far ahead the thrush is seen;
Here along the southern wall
Keeps the bee his festival;
All is quiet else – afar
Sounds of toil and turmoil are.

Here be shadows large and long;
Here be spaces meet for song;
Grant, O garden-god, that I,
Now that mood and moment please, –
Find the fair Pierides!

Broadfield Court
The house is an intriguing mixture of architectural styles facing the formal gardens, which lead into a more extensive area of old English gardens, and the vineyard of Bodenham English Wines.
Please see entry in Index and Gazetteer.

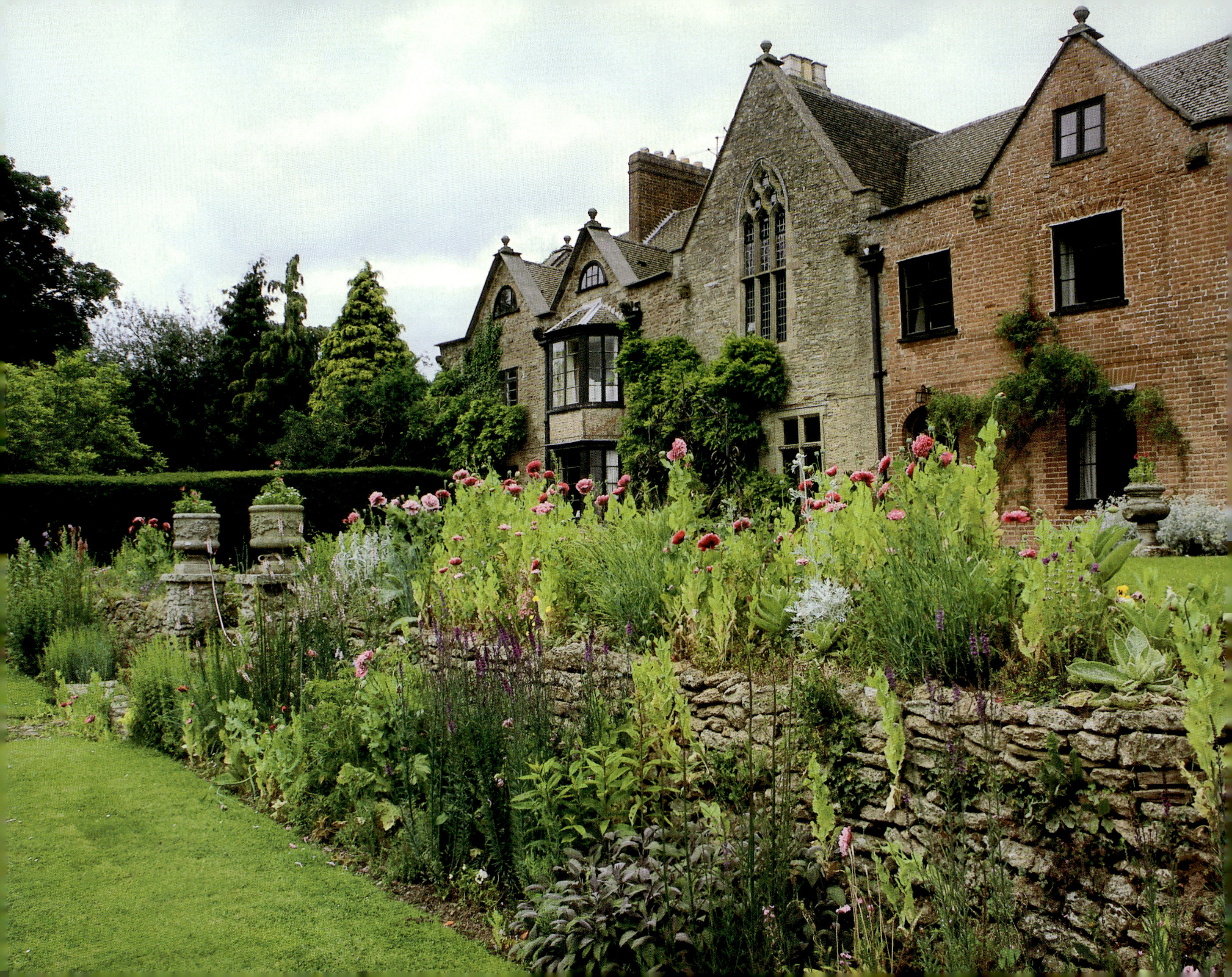

Thaw

EDWARD THOMAS

Over the land freckled with snow half-thawed
The speculating rooks at their nests cawed
And saw from elm-tops, delicate as flower of grass,
What we below could not see, Winter pass.

WINTER CONTRASTS

Left: A lovely frosted landscape on a dull winter morning at Pigmore Common near Eardisland.

Opposite: Bright sunshine after an overnight snowfall on fields near Pembridge.

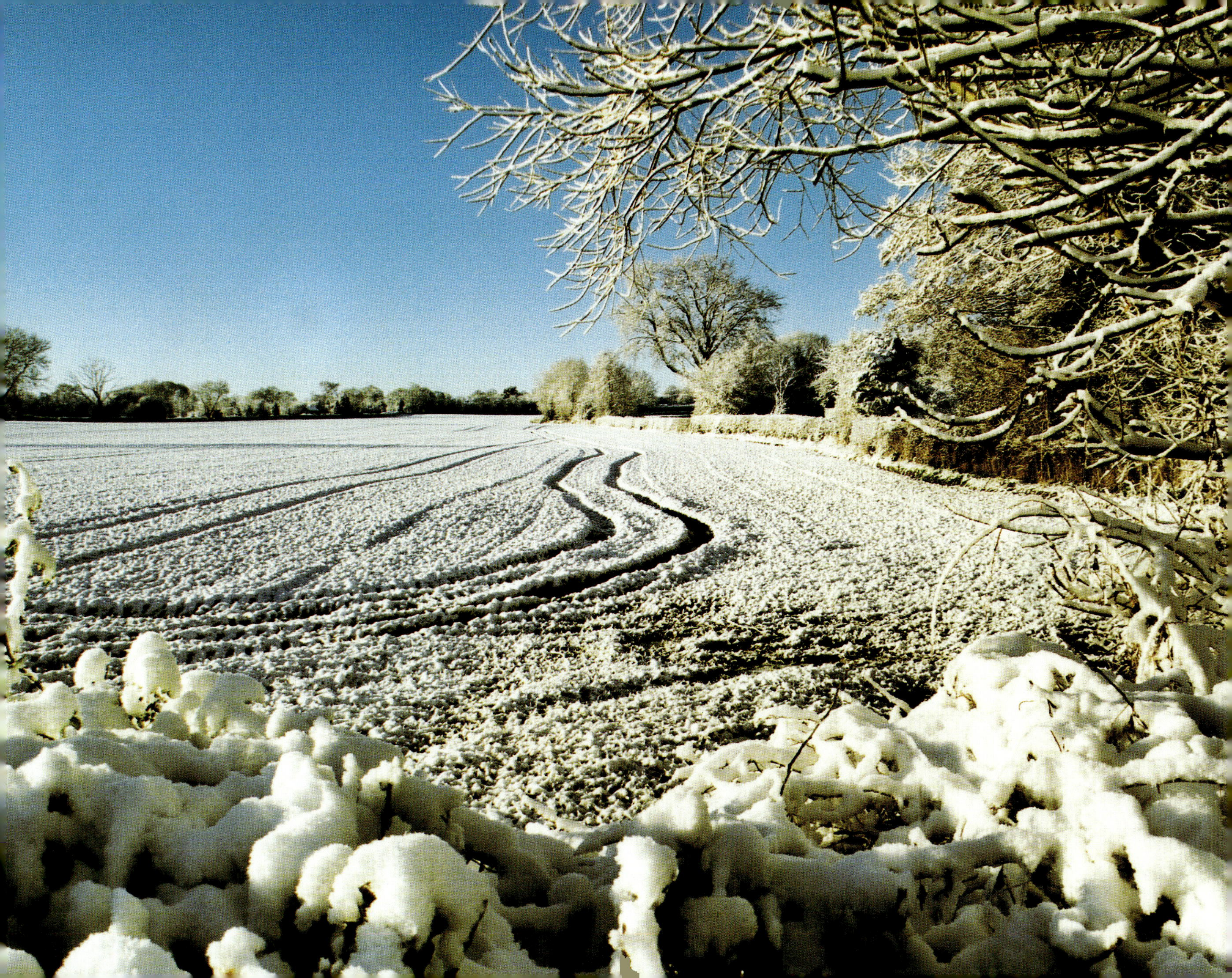

HEREFORDSHIRE BRIDGES ENHANCE THE LANDSCAPE AND ADD ARCHITECTURAL INTEREST TO ANY JOURNEY.

Above: Kerne Bridge. Facing page: Whitney Toll Bridge. Overleaf: Bredwardine Bridge and the avenue leading from Bredwardine church.

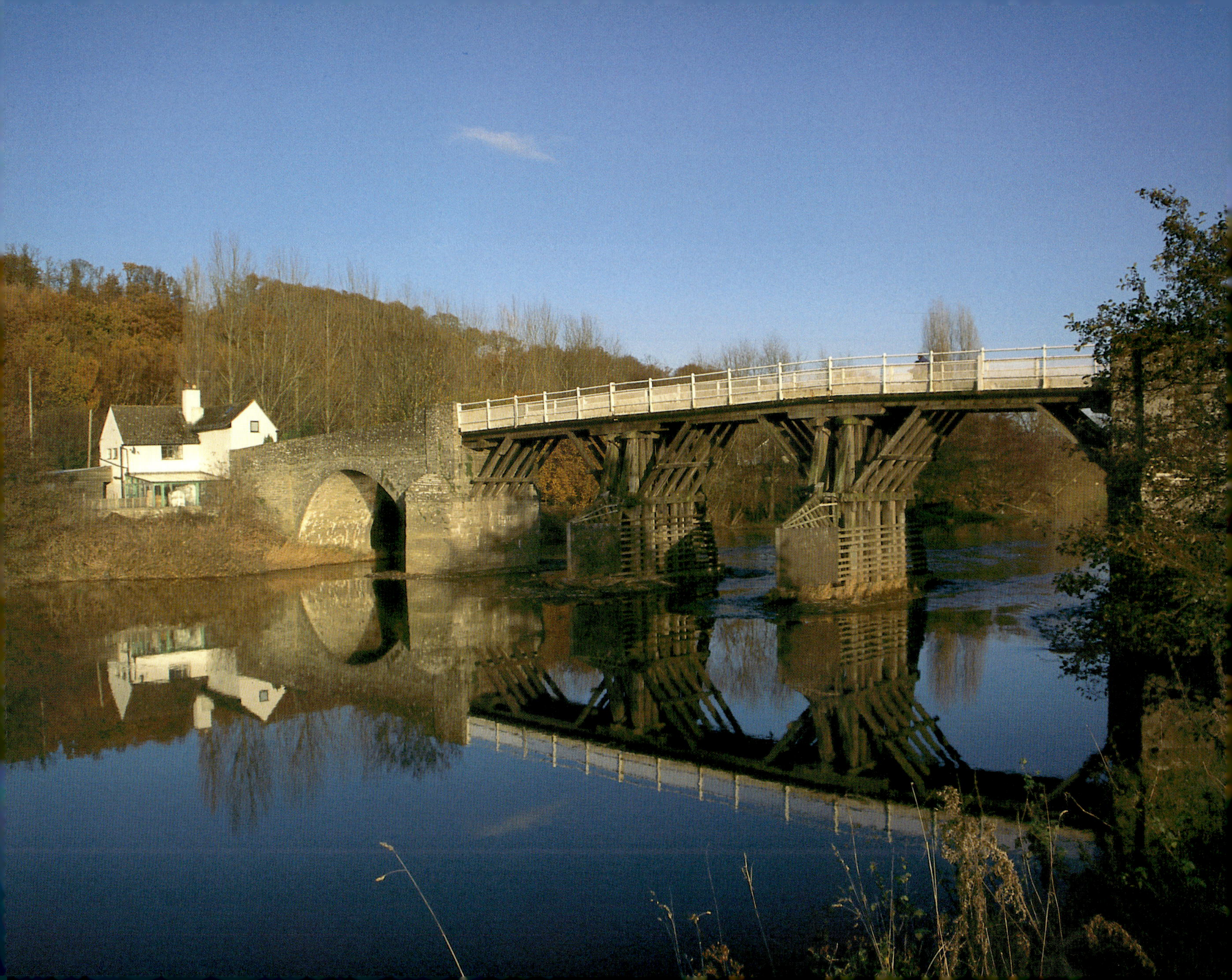

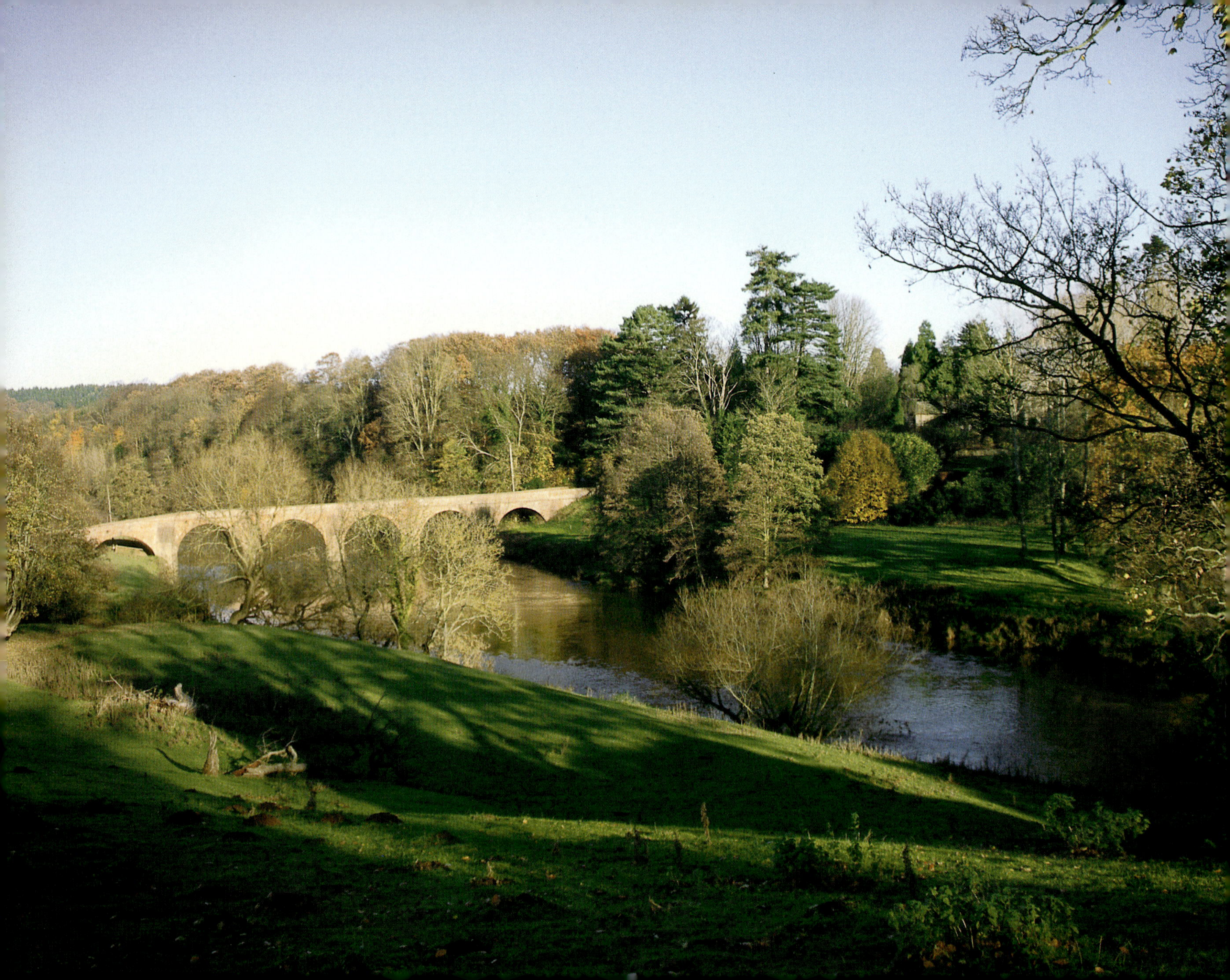

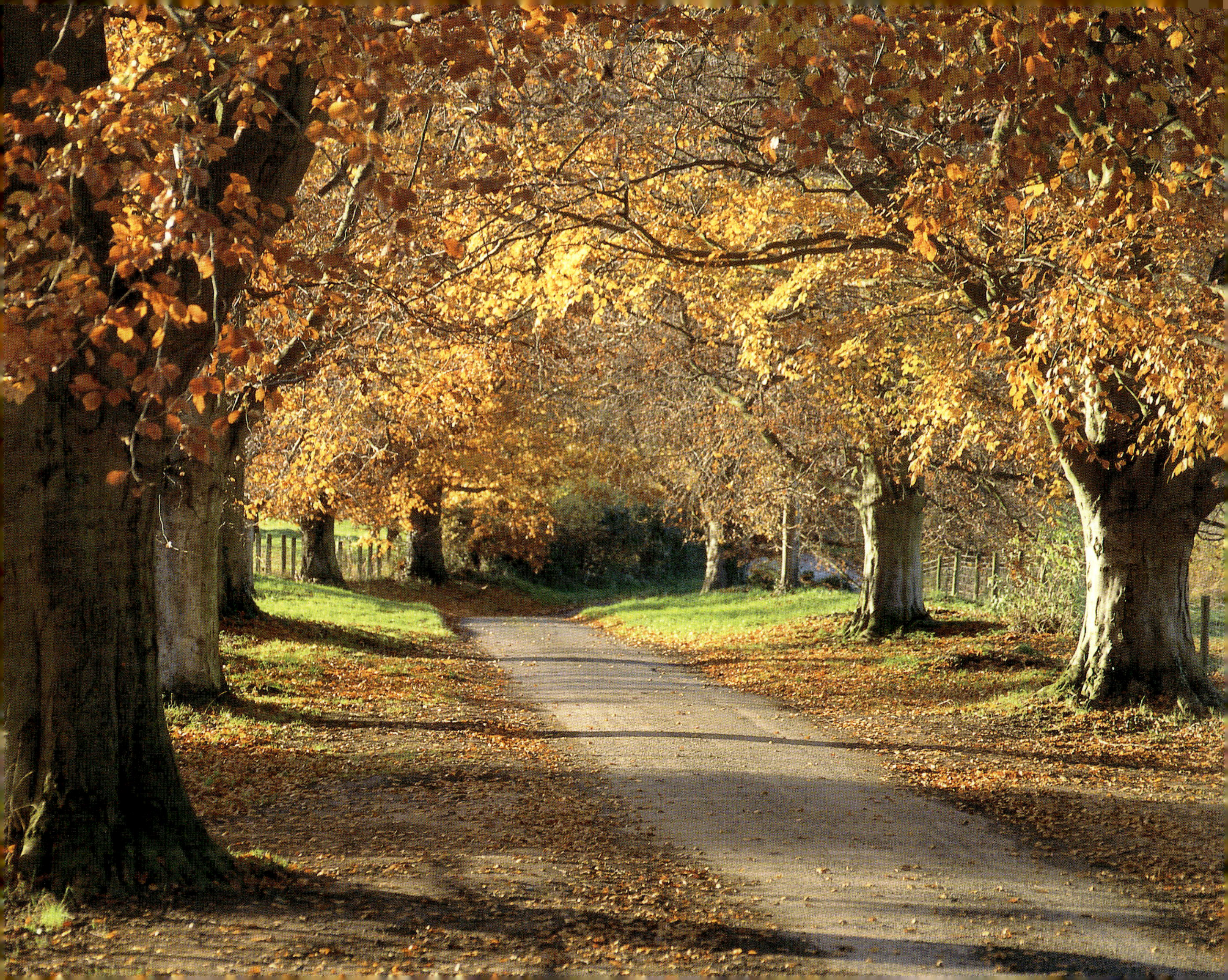

The Road not Taken
ROBERT FROST

Two roads diverged in a yellow wood,
And sorry I could not travel both
And be one traveller, long I stood
And looked down one as far as I could
To where it bent in the undergrowth;

Then took the other, as just as fair,
And having perhaps the better claim,
Because it was grassy and wanted wear;
Though as for that the passing there
Had worn them really about the same,

And both that morning equally lay
In leaves no step had trodden black.
Oh, I kept the first for another day!
Yet knowing how way leads on to way,
I doubted if I should ever come back.

I shall be telling this with a sigh
Somewhere ages and ages hence;
Two roads diverged in a wood, and I –
I took the one less travelled by,
And that has made all the difference.

Quiet Country Roads
Above: A crossroads near Bromyard
Facing page: A road near Dilwyn in late autumn sunshine.

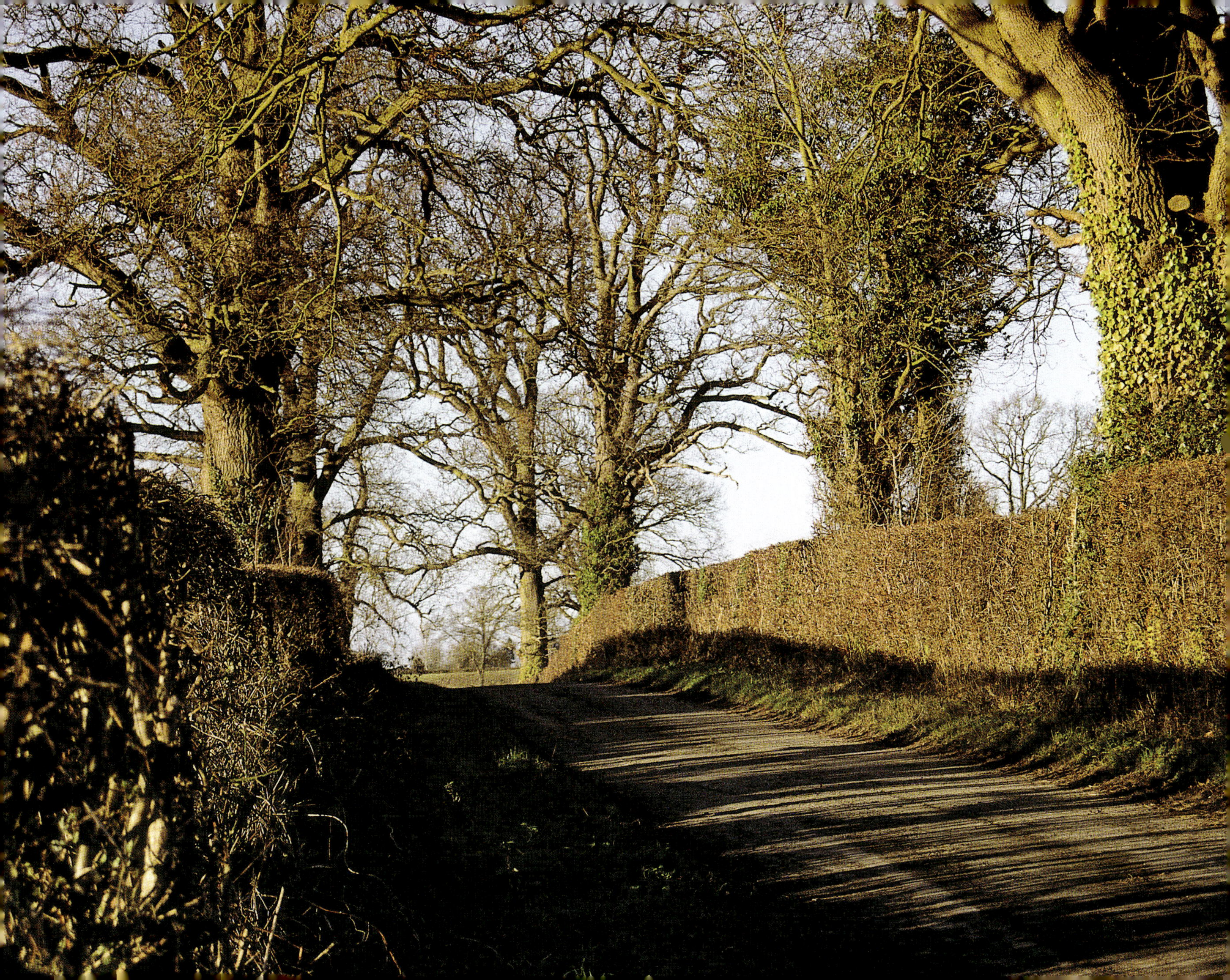

Ode on Solitude

ALEXANDER POPE

Happy the man, whose wish and care
A few paternal acres bound,
Content to breathe his native air
In his own ground

Whose herds with milk, whose fields with bread,
Whose flocks supply him with attire:
Whose trees in summer yield him shade,
In winter, fire.

Blest, who can unconcern'dly find
Hours, days, and years, slide soft away
In health of body, peace of mind,
Quiet by day.

Sound sleep at night; study and ease
Together mixt, sweet recreation.
And innocence, which most does please
With meditation.

Thus let me live, unseen, unknown;
Thus unlamented let me die;
Steal from the world, and not a stone
Tell where I lie.

Opposite page: Cottage in East Herefordshire looking towards the Malverns.
I saw this cottage as a microcosm of the landscape: its pinkish brick walls and blue-grey roof mirrored the wider landscape, making the cottage seem an integral part of the countryside rather than an imposed man-made structure.

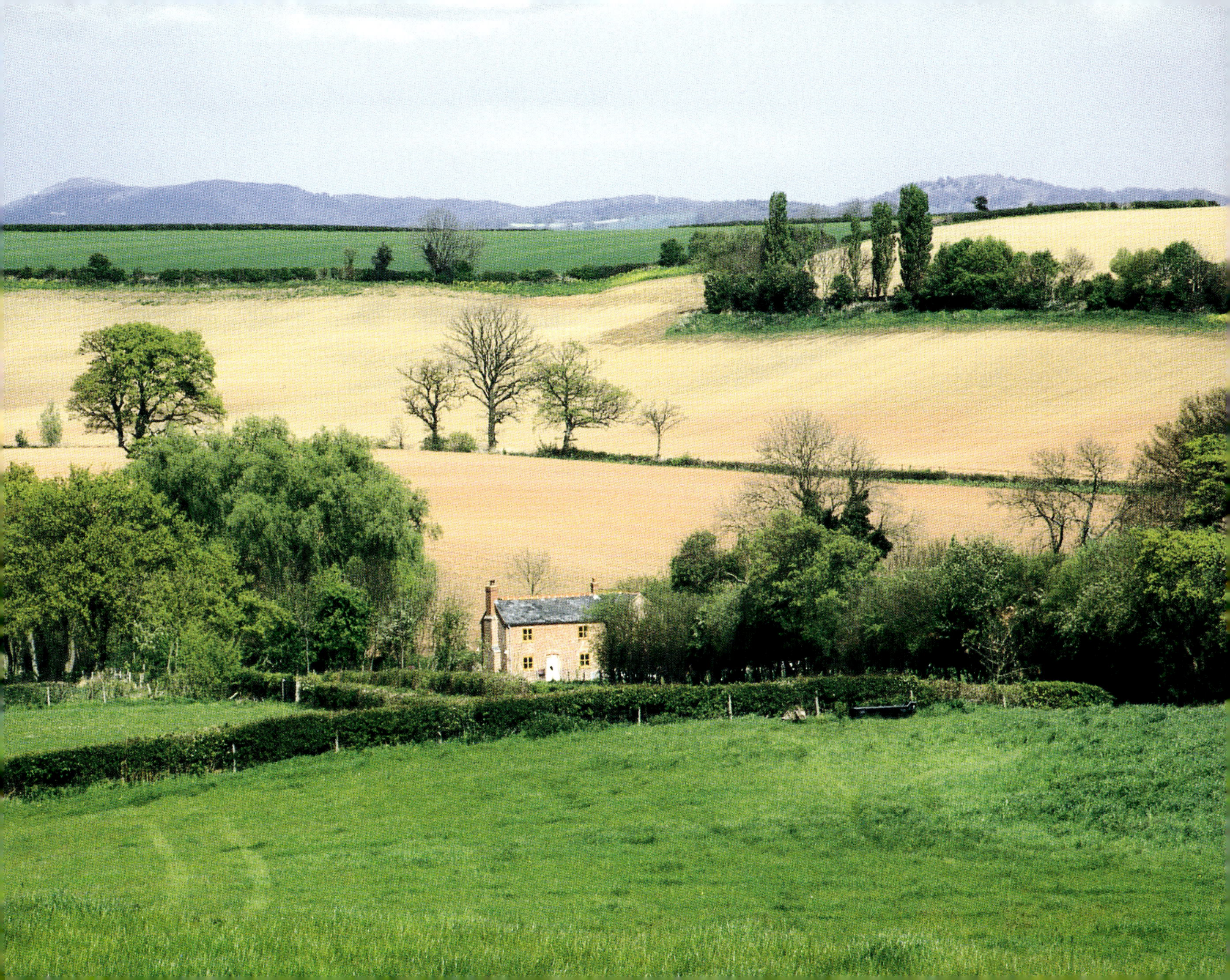

GARDENS COME IN INFINITE VARIETY.

Above: The entrance to a house at Evesbatch. Facing page: A riot of spring colours outside The Old Smithy, Eardisland.

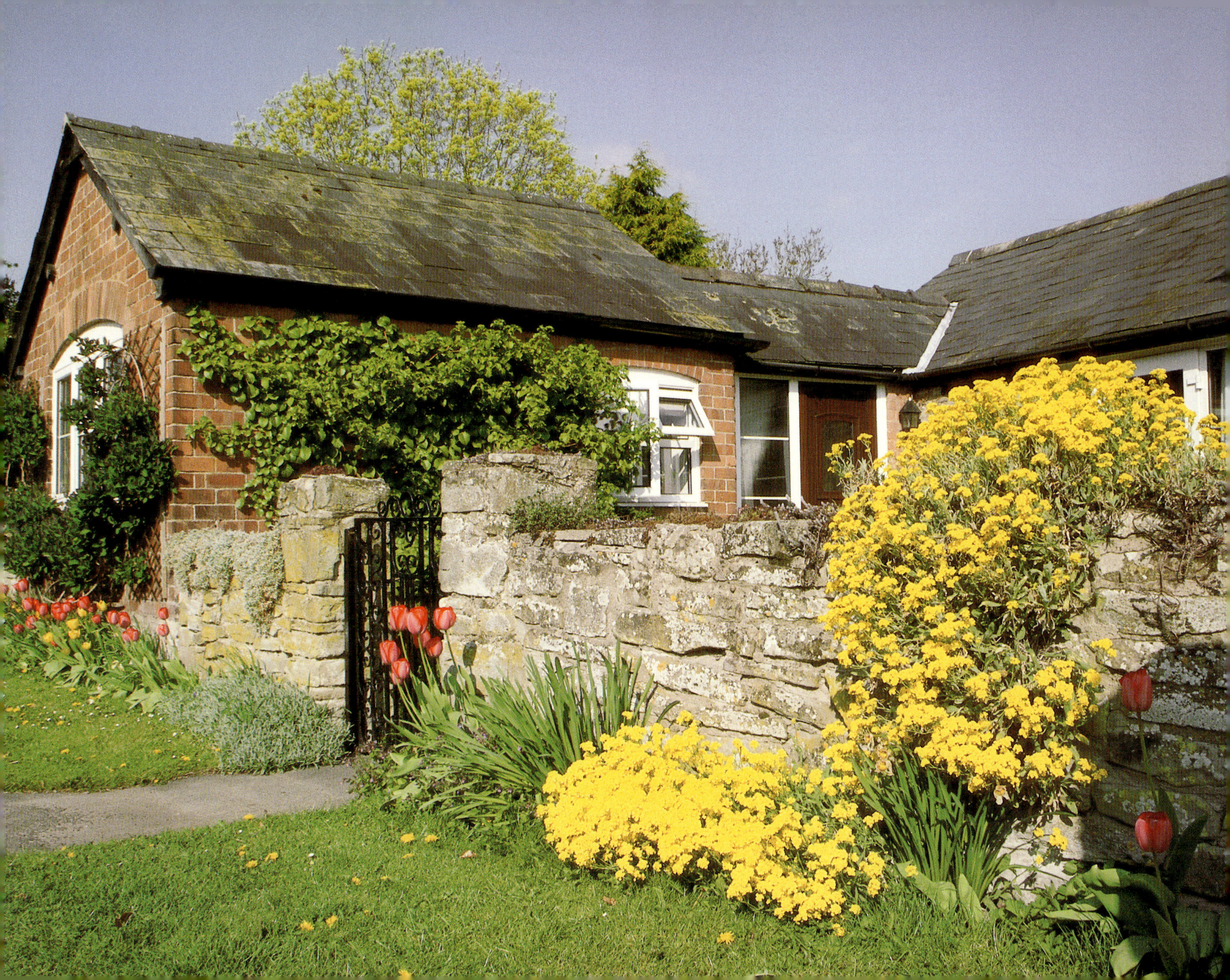

Sonnet Eighteen

William Shakespeare

Shall I compare thee to a summer's day?
Thou are more lovely and more temperate.
Rough winds do shake the darling buds of May,
And summer's lease hath all too short a date:
Sometime too hot the eye of heaven shines,
And often is his gold complexion dimm'd;
And every fair from fair sometime declines,
By chance, or nature's changing course, untrimmed;
But thy eternal summer shall not fade,
Not lose possession of that fair thy ow'st;
Nor shall Death brag thou wander'st in his shade.
When in eternal lines to time thou grow'st.
So long as men can breathe, or eyes can see,
So long lives this, and this gives life to thee.

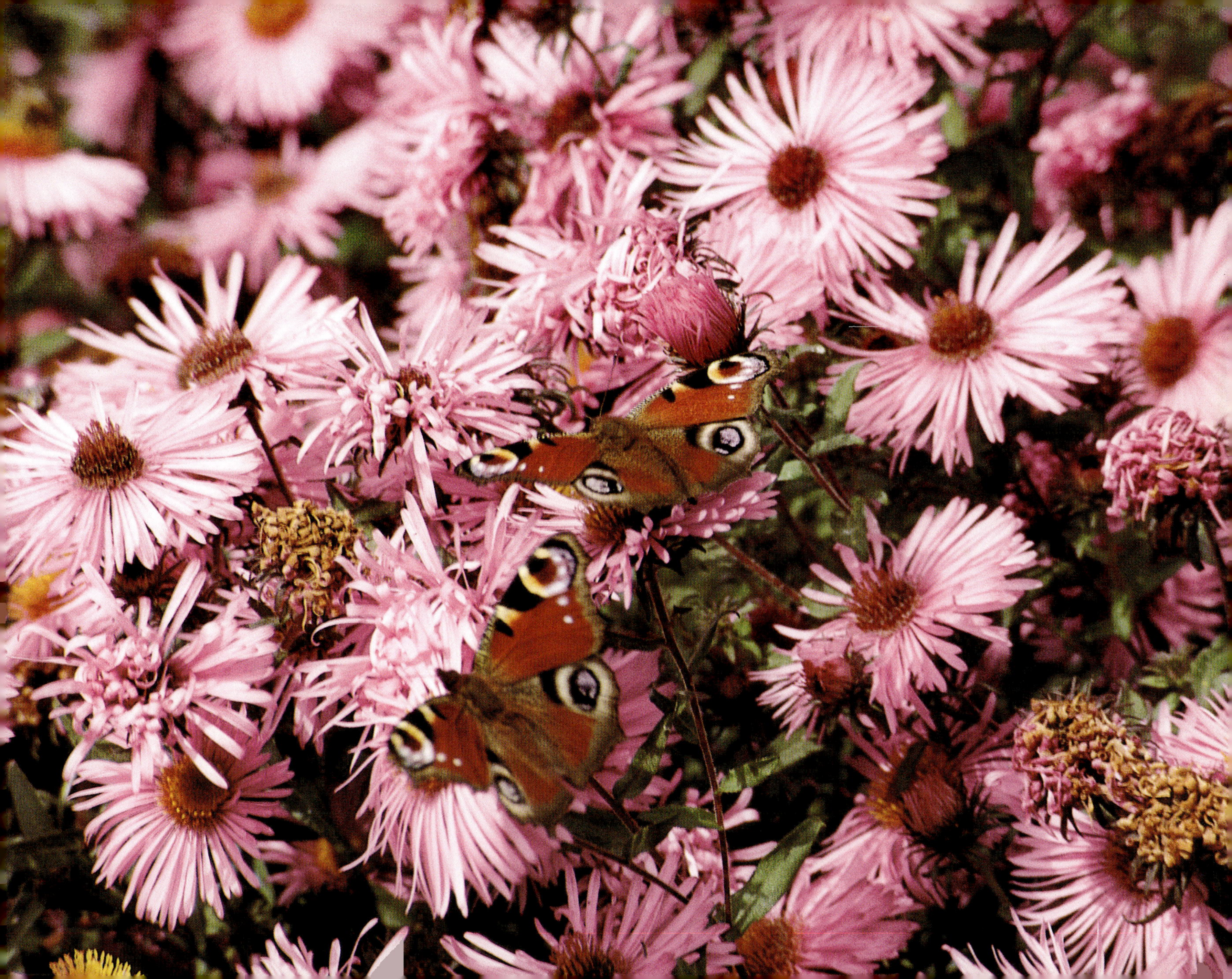

Ploughing up the Pasture
Margaret Stanley-Wrench

Now up the pasture's slope the ploughed land laps
In folds that fall and crumble from the share.
Rooks drop to the warm earth, hot leather creaks,
The sweat of labouring flesh steams in the air.
The flanks of beast are smooth with sun and toil.
The cropped turves that are worn with years of grazing
Turn inwards to the steel, and over the long
Acres of grassland stretch the ribs of soil.
No longer when in summer the clotted shadows
Fall from the crest of trees, will they stretch over
The lazy turf, but will shadow a new world
Of yellow acres, fret and stir of meadows,
Green barley, freckled silver by the wind.
And corn like a fresh sea across the world.

Ploughing with horses makes an attractive scene at agricultural society competitions … provided you only have to do half-a-dozen furrows. In reality it was back-breaking, hand-numbing, unremitting toil. As the picture opposite shows, beautiful geometric patterns can be created by modern ploughing with infinitely less discomfort, and in a fraction of the time.

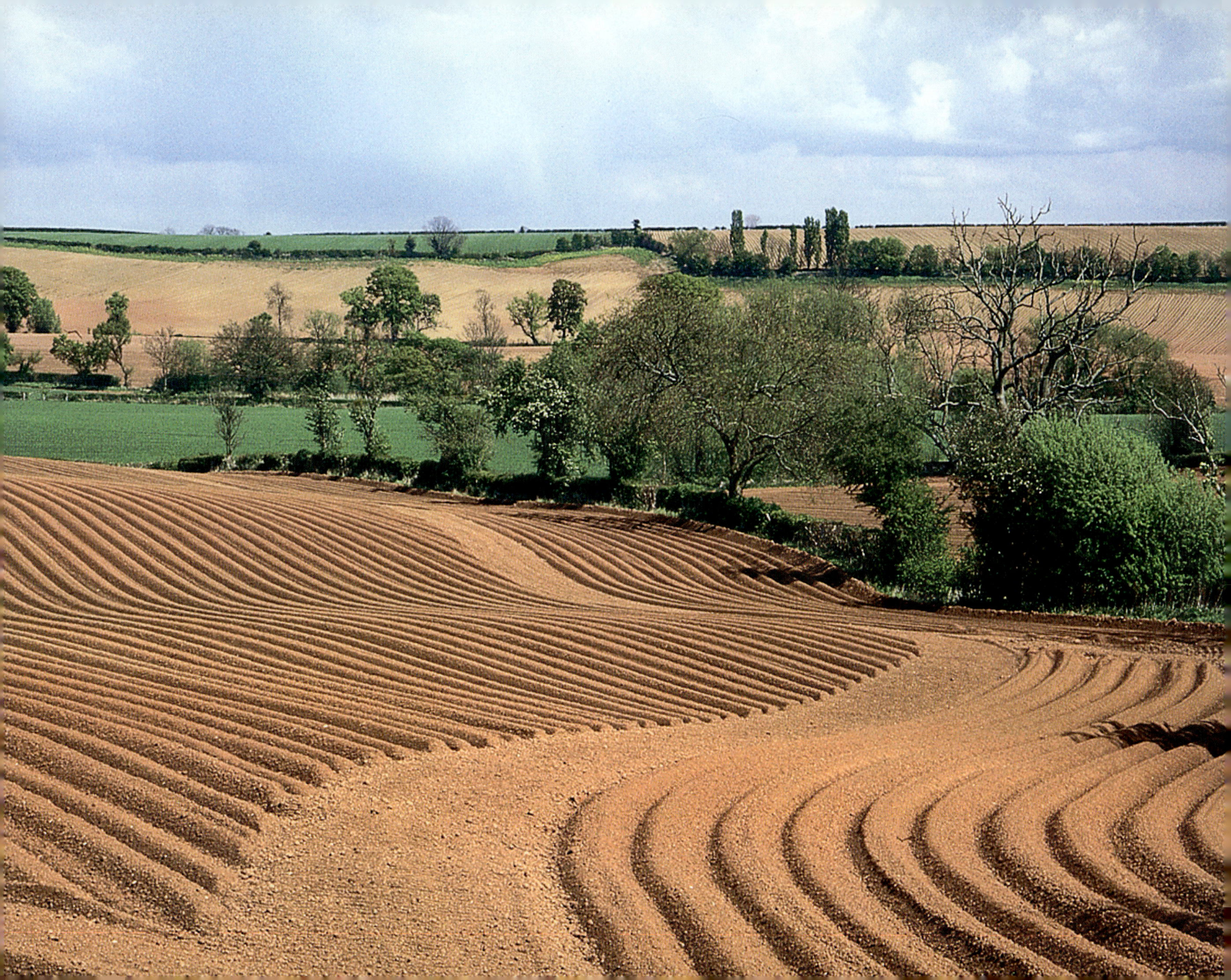

Meg Merrilies

JOHN KEATS

Old Meg she was a gipsy;
And lived upon the moors:
Her bed it was the brown heath turf,
And her house was out of doors.

Her apples were swart blackberries,
Her currants pods o' broom;
Her wine was dew of the wild white rose,
Her book a churchyard tomb.

Her brothers were the craggy hills,
Her sisters larchen trees;
Alone with her great family
She lived as she did please.

No breakfast had she many a morn,
No dinner many a noon,
And 'stead of supper she would stare
Full hard against the moon.

But every morn of woodbine fresh
She made her garlanding,
And every night the dark glen yew
She wove, and she would sing.

And with her fingers old and brown
She plaited mats o' rushes,
And gave them to the cottagers
She met among the bushes.

Old Meg was brave as Margaret Queen,
And tall as Amazon;
An old red blanket cloak she wore,
A chip hat had she on.
God rest her aged bones somewhere;
She died full long agone.

I have known this poem since I answered questions on it in my Eng.Lit. O level exam. When I recently lost my way on a footpath in the Goodrich area, I came across this old, wooden, half-painted caravan at the edge of a wood. I thought it would provide the ideal complement for the Meg Merrilies poem, which I was determined to include in this book.

A sensitive company rep., (such a person does exist), said to me when he saw a proof print, "Couldn't you just imagine yourself there, where nobody could get at you?" I thought, my sentiments exactly: a secret bolt hole when life gets too hectic and you need time to sit and think (or just sit!). Dream on!

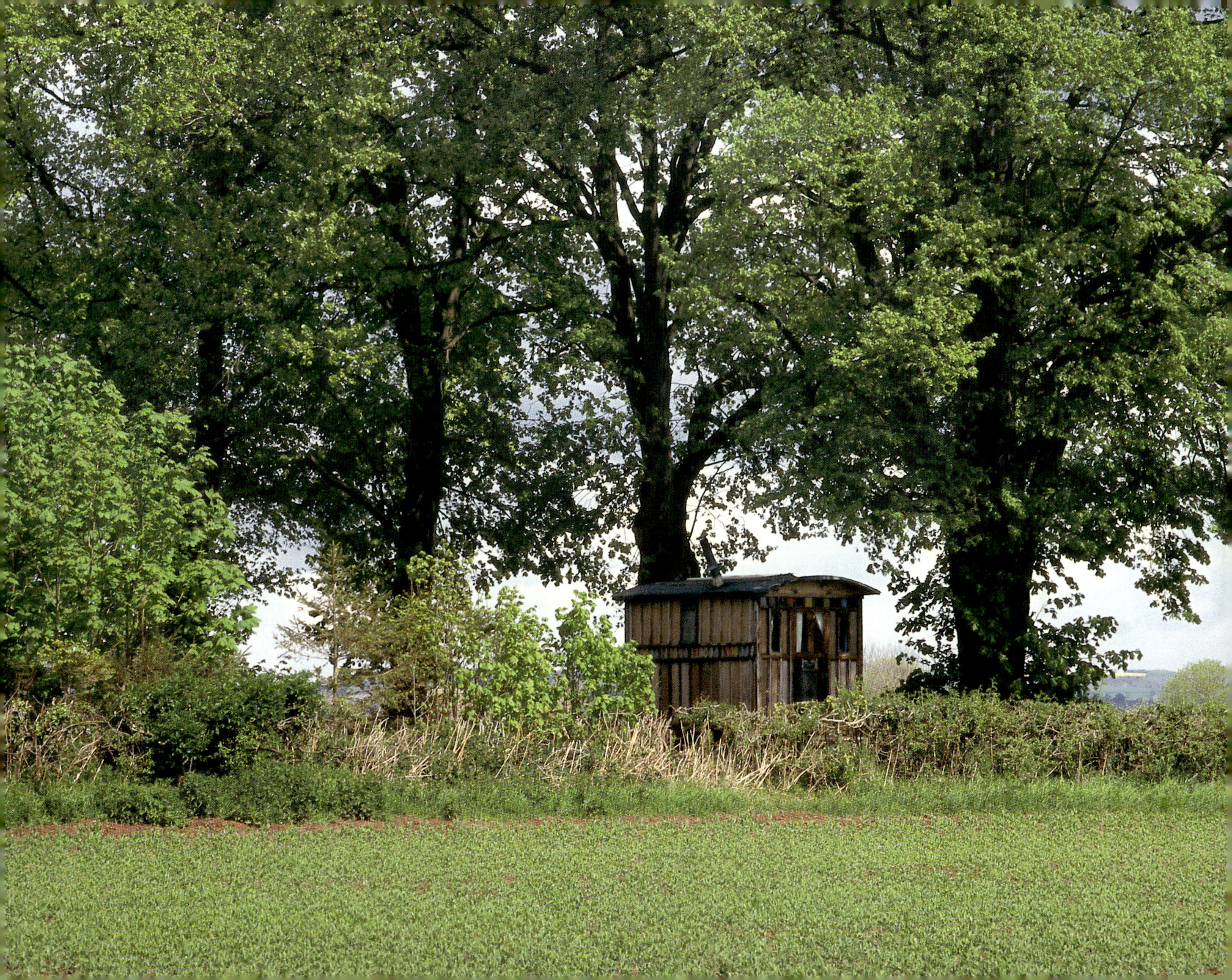

A Birthday

Christina Georgina Rossetti

My heart is like a singing bird
Whose nest is in a watered shoot;
My heart is like an apple-tree
Whose boughs are bent with thickset fruit;
My heart is like a rainbow shell
That paddles in a halcyon sea;
My heart is gladder than all these
Because my love is come to me.

Raise me a dais of silk and down;
Hang it with vair and purple dyes;
Carve it in doves and pomegranates,
And peacocks with a hundred eyes;
Work it in gold and silver grapes,
In leaves and silver fleur-de-lys;
Because the birthday of my life
Is come, my love is come to me.

Lupins in a cottage garden at Bodenham.

Remember

Christina Georgina Rossetti

Remember me when I am gone away,
Gone far away into the silent land;
When you can no more hold me by the hand,
Nor I half turn to go yet turning stay.
Remember me when no more day by day
You tell me of our future that you planned:
Only remember me; you understand
It will be late to counsel then or pray.
Yet if you should forget me for a while
And afterwards remember, do not grieve:
For if the darkness and corruption leave
A vestige of the thoughts that once I had.
Better by far you should forget and smile
Than that you should remember and be sad.

On Bircher Common

The Life that I Have

Leo Marks

The life that I have
Is all that I have
And the life that I have
Is yours

The love that I have
Of the life that I have
Is yours and yours and yours

A sleep I shall have
A rest I shall have
Yet death will be but a pause

For the peace of my years
In the long green grass
Will be yours and yours and yours

Rosemary Rigby MBE

Raising huge sums for the RNIB is the achievement for which Rosemary Rigby has been deservedly honoured, but it is her determination to provide a permanent memorial to the wartime SOE agent, Violette Szabo GC, that will in fact stand as Rosemary's own enduring memorial.

Rosemary lives in the house at Wormelow where Violette spent happy childhood holidays, and continued to visit right up to her last mission, which ended with her murder in Ravensbruck in 1945. By inspiring others, including Virginia McKenna who played Violette in *Carve her Name with Pride*, and by sheer determination, Rosemary finally saw her dream of a museum realised. Booked parties and hundreds of individuals are now finding their way to this quiet country garden where the young woman, whom fellow SOE agent, Odette Churchill, called "the bravest of us all", spent the carefree summers of the 1930's.

I had met Rosemary on previous occasions, but arrived on her doorstep, unannounced, on my way back from south Herefordshire one summer evening. When I asked if I might take some portrait shots of her, she immediately responded with her characteristic charm and patience.

Thank you, Rosemary. You are determined we should be proud of Violette Szabo. All of us in Herefordshire should be proud to have you in our midst.

Please see entry in Index and Gazetteer.

The Life that I Have: this poem became well known world-wide when *Carve Her Name With Pride* was released to cinemas in 1958. It was a coding poem written by Leo Marks, the Head of Codes for Special Operations Executive. Lines from the poem have been used as the headings for a series of display boards in the Violette Szabo G.C. Museum.

The photograph above shows Rosemary Rigby in a corner of the museum. The portrait opposite shows Rosemary sitting in her garden at Wormelow: the path behind her leads to the museum which can just be seen in the background.

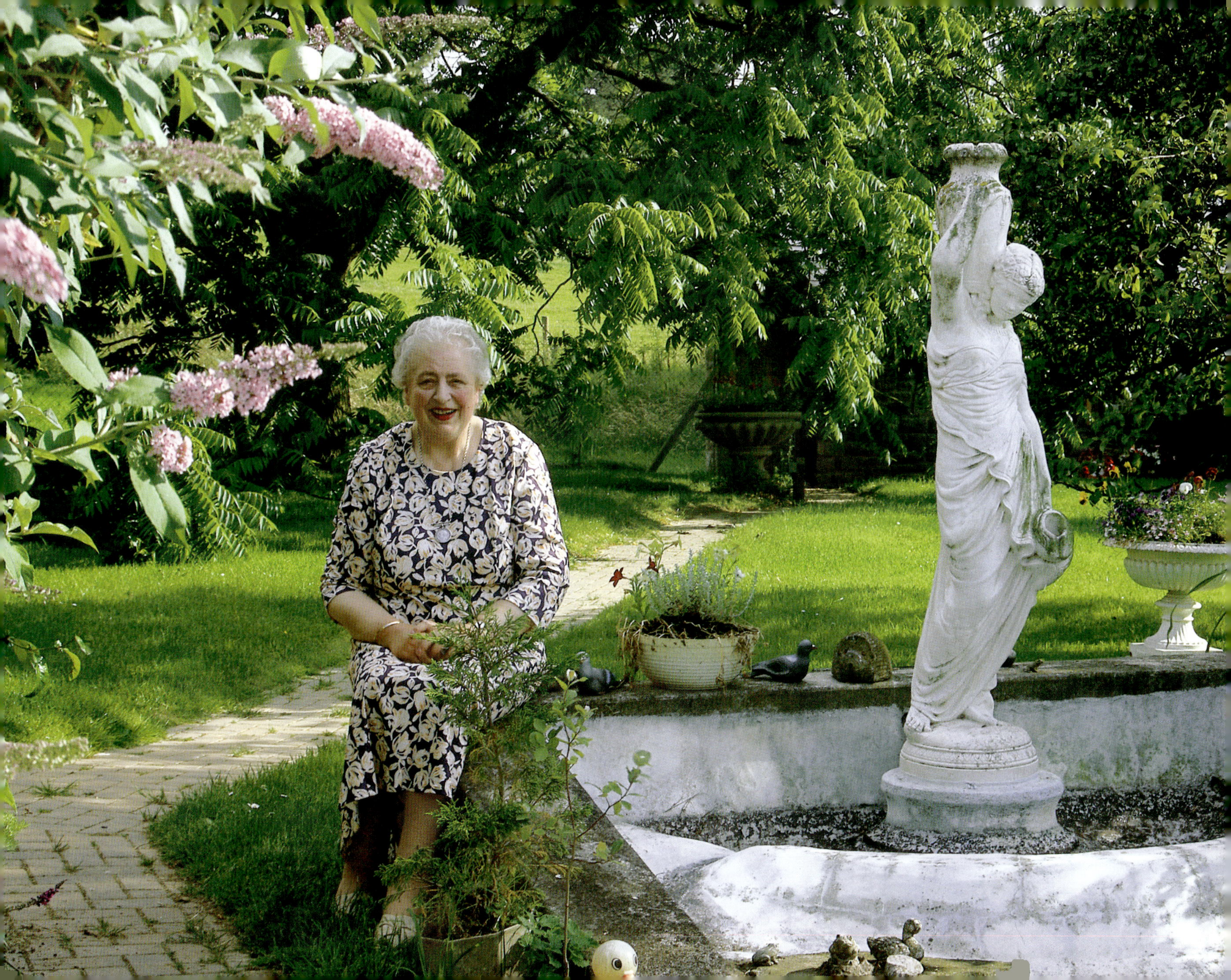

The Gate of the Year
M. Louise Haskins

And I said to the man who stood at the gate of the year:
'Give me a light, that I may tread safely into the unknown!'
And he replied:
'Go out into the darkness and put your hand into the Hand of God.
That shall be to you better than light and safer than a known way.'

So, I went forth, and finding the Hand of God, trod gladly into the night
And He led me toward the hills and the breaking of day in the lone East.

So, heart, be still!
What need our little life,
Our human life, to know,
If God hath comprehension?
In all the dizzy strife
Of things both high and low
God hideth His intention.

At the Turn of the Year
Afternoon sunshine on the River Arrow in late December.

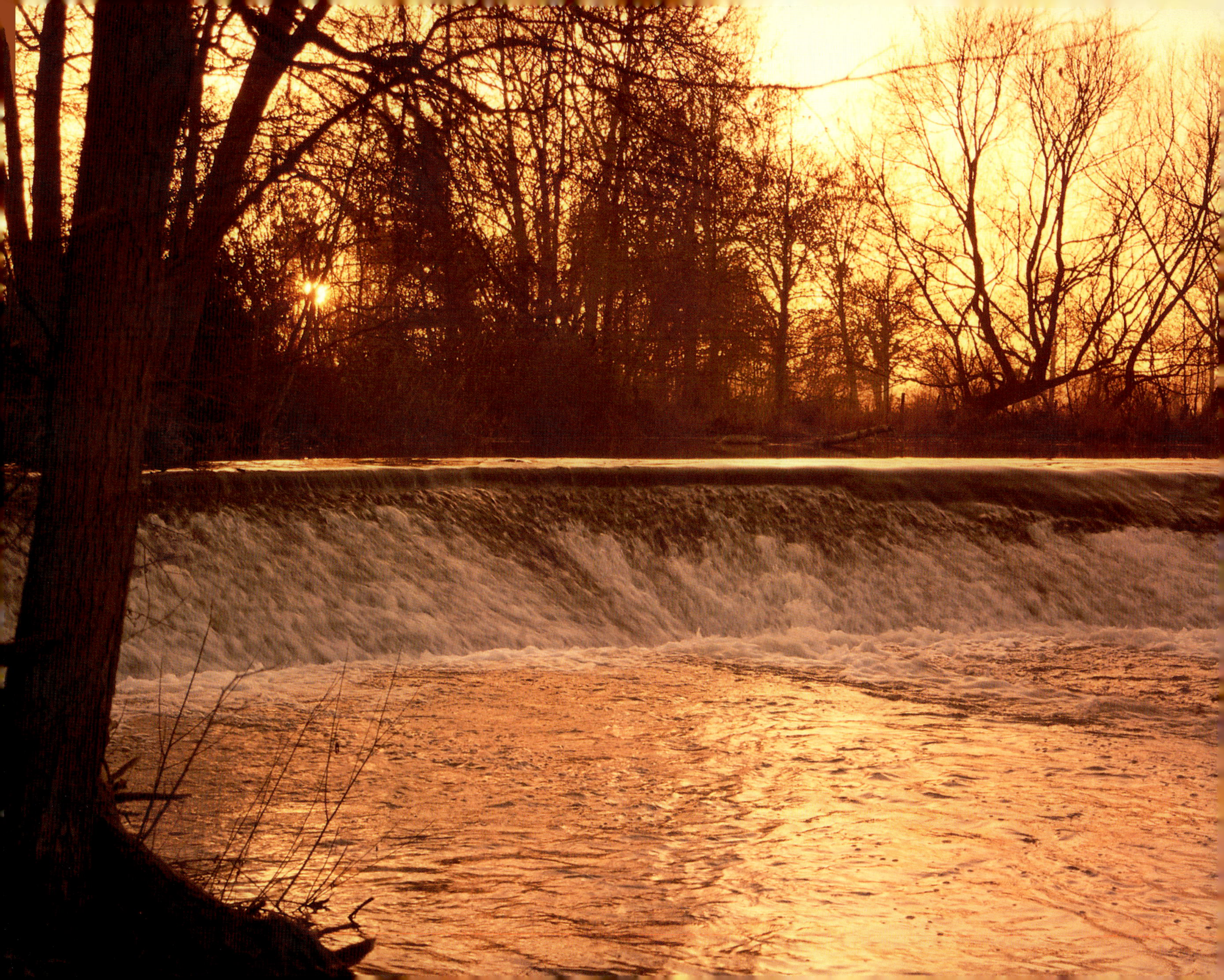

Arrow Valley Publications

Eardisland

Kathleen and Barry Freeman formed Arrow Valley Publications early in 1999 to create beautiful books and, in the process, to generate funds for hospices and other charities. To date, almost £10,000 has been raised.

Each book is essentially a co-operative effort. Kathleen and Barry count themselves fortunate that they have complementary interests which can be combined to create these books, which have become so popular. Kathleen of course takes the pictures and, in the case of this book, has written the majority of the text. Barry chose the poems, and created the general layout of the book. On some excursions he has been honorary chauffeur and tea maker!

Arrow Valley Publications is based at Eardisland Tea Room, opposite the church in the centre of this renowned village. As well as the tea room, there is also a fascinating book, card and gift shop, and a delightful garden to sit in when the weather is appropriate. Kathleen and Barry are always pleased to meet customers and have a chat on the quieter days.

For all enquiries about the books or tea room, the contact details are: Arrow Valley Publications, Church Lane, Eardisland, near Leominster, Herefordshire, HR6 9BP. Telephone 01544 388226

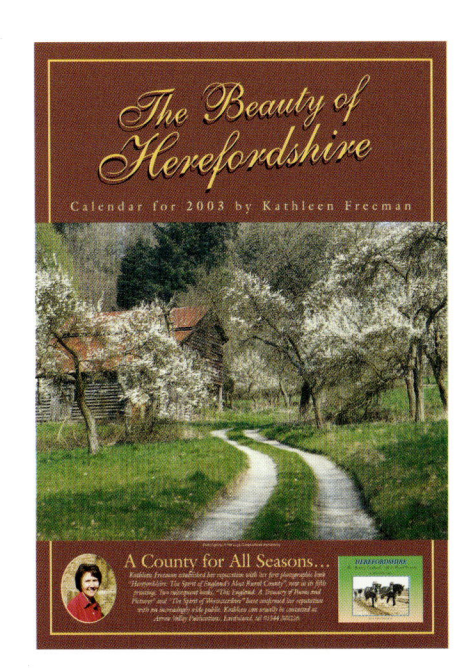

The Pictures

Far left: Kathleen and Barry in their tea room.

Below: the books and calendars. (Both photos courtesy of Hereford Times: photographer, David Griffiths).

Left: the 2003 calendar, available from selected shops and our tea room.

Right: the view from Arrow Valley Publications office, through the garden to Eardisland church.

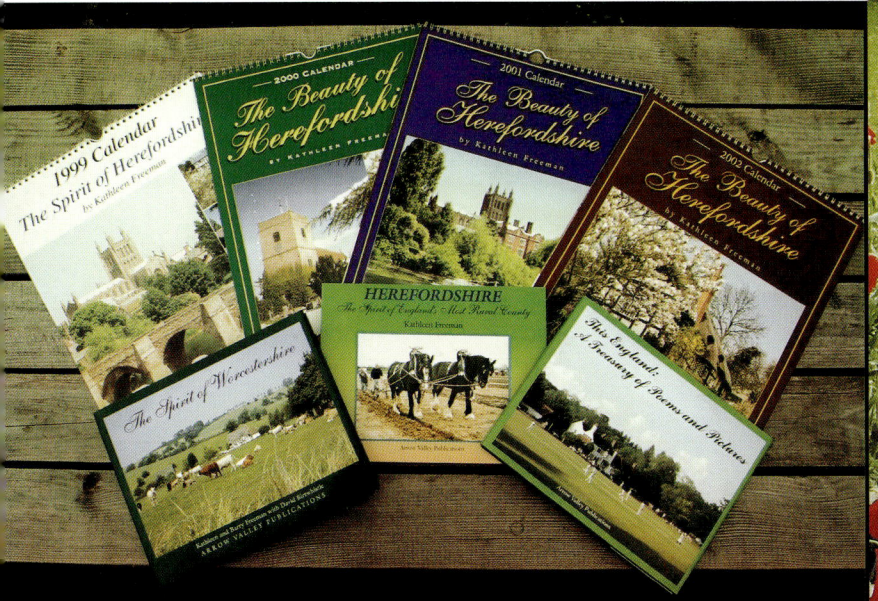

Index of Photographic Locations

Arrow Valley: 12, 92, 114
Aymestrey: 16

Bircher Common: 111
Black Mountains: 8, 37
Bodenham: 87, 110
Bollitree Castle: 48
Bredwardine: 56, 94
Breinton: 14
Broadfield Court: 90
Bromyard area: 12, 30, 82, 98

Dilwyn area: 98
Dinmore Manor: 80
Dulas: 80

Eardisland: 56, 62, 102
Eastnor: 18
Evesbatch: 72, 102

Frome Valley: 34, 78, 88

Garway Hill: 62
Goodrich area: 20, 28, 54, 108
Gorsley Common: 84

Hampton Court: 40, 50
Hereford: 22
Hergest Croft: 68
Hope Mansell: 56

Kentchurch: 26, 70
Kerne Bridge: 10, 94
Kimbolton: 64

Ledbury: 33
Leominster: 74
Linton Hill: 46, 84
Lugg Valley: 16
Lyonshall: 66

Malverns: 34
Mayhill: 24
Monnow Valley: 58, 60

Ocle Pychard: 64

Ross-on-Wye: 46
Rowlestone: 76

Titley: 37, 66

Walterstone: 58
Weston-under-Penyard: 46
Westonbury Mill: 44
Whitney Toll Bridge: 94
Wormelow: 112

Gazetteer

The following places were visited during the course of preparing this book, and are open to the public. The details provided here are believed to be correct at the time of printing (autumn 2002), but please check with the establishments or a Tourist Information Office.

(Page 7) Frome Valley Vineyard, Paunton Court near Bishops Frome. Tel: 01885 490735. Wine tasting and sales in ancient threshing barn leading out to a model vineyard. Open April to October, Wednesday to Sunday, 11am to 5pm.

(Page 26) Barton Hill Animal Centre, Kentchurch. Tel: 01981 240749
Delightful animal sanctuary set on a hillside and in farm buildings; pigs and donkeys are especially endearing, plus a range of ponies, rabbits and other animals. Open April to September.

(Page 40) Hampton Court Gardens, Hope under Dinmore. Tel: 01568 797777
Superb gardens, parkland, riverside and woodland walks; restaurant and shop. A major new attraction: special event days. Open late March to late December from 11am daily.

(Page 44) Westonbury Mill Water Garden, 3 miles west of Pembridge, on A44. Tel: 01544 388650
Huge variety of moisture-loving plants in a tangle of streams and ponds, plus unusual water features. Open summer weekends and Bank Holidays 11am to 5pm.

(Page 58) The Cellar Gallery, Grove Farm, Walterstone. Tel: 01873 890293
Permanent exhibition of paintings by Christine Hunt on a hill farm overlooking the Monnow Valley and Black Mountains: superb views. Open most days: signposted off A465 Hereford to Abergavenny road by Old Pandy inn.

(Page 68) Hergest Croft Gardens, Kington. Tel: 230160
Magnificent, long-established gardens, over 50 acres: thousands of trees and shrubs. Tea rooms and special events. Open late March to end October.

(Page 91) Bodenham English Wines, Broadfield Court, near Bodenham, off A417. Tel: 01568 797483
Domesday manor house with 5 acres of traditional English gardens and 14 acres of vineyards. Wine tasting and gift shop; tea room open in summer. Open April to October 10am to 4pm; shop only October to April.

(Page 112) The Violette Szabo GC Museum, Wormelow. Tel: 01981 540477
A moving memorial to one of England's bravest agents, executed at Ravensbruck in January 1945, and made world-famous in the film *Carve Her Name with Pride*. Open Wednesdays, April to October; other times and groups by appointment.

Tiger: Obit August 2000

Like me, Tiger loved country walks. For ten years or more he plodded faithfully behind me through the fields outside Eardisland. He always ran ahead and sat on the parapet of this little bridge.

Happy exploring in Herefordshire … especially along the small, unsignposted roads!